WEIGHTLIFTING
Strength and Velocity

Weightlifting
Strength & Velocity

About the Author

 Born 1945 in Wichita Falls, Texas, and grew up in Fort Worth, Texas. Graduated from Arlington Heights High School in 1963. Was captain of the track team and placed second at the Texas State Meet in the Discus in 1963. Attended Howard County Junior College on an athletic scholarship and placed second in the Junior College Nationals in the discus in 1964 and 1965. Attended TCU on an athletic scholarship. Received a degree in Physical Education in 1968, taking courses in (physics, statistics, biology, kinesiology and Anatomy). National Weightlifting Champion in 1977 in the 82.5 kg class and placed second at Nationals in 1975, 1976 and 1978. Set four American records in the snatch, including a Pan American Record snatch of 140 kg in the 75 kg class, American Record

snatch 142.5 in the 75 kg class in 1978, and National record snatch of 155 kg in the 82.5 kg class in 1979. Set National and World Record in masters division.

Jim has been a member of Spoon Barbell Club Weightlifting Team since 1974. Inducted into Texas Weightlifting Hall of Fame 2009.

Table of Content

Section 1: Mechanics of Motion

In athletics, it is necessary to increase the efficiency of the mechanics of motion through particular changes in accelerated velocity (momentum), using the athlete's own particular physiology and within the rules governing those sports or event(s). The rules governing the athlete's sport or event(s) determines the sufficiency of technique. Proficiency of technique is arrived at through the athlete's ability to produce the necessary momentum, within the rules, in order to achieve the best result.

Technique is "a skillful or an efficient way of doing or achieving something".

"Efficient" is the key word in the definition of technique. The word "skillful" is non-specific, just as good, excellent, great, perfect and other similar descriptors of technique are non-specific, regarding any particular type of technique used in athletics.

Efficient: Achieving maximum productivity with a minimum of wasted motion or time. For an athlete to become exceptionally skillful they need to be able to perform their event at maximal effort (velocity), by eliminating all unnecessary motions.

Where technique is concerned, the most important element is whether or not that technique is within close tolerance levels of the technical skills and velocities of the top lifters in the world. Performances are advanced through a system of trial and error and evolution, so to speak. It does little good for a lifter to try and copy another lifter's technique if the lifter being copied has not reached a high level of proficiency.

Weightlifting requires the athlete to both produce force and overcome force in order to maintain those specific accelerated velocities which can be used to complete a lift. Technique must include specific accelerated velocities and not just the mechanics of motion concerned with the events.

Points for style are not awarded to a lifter, as points are awarded in the sports of diving, ice skating, ski jumping or gymnastics. A lifter spending more time in an effort trying to achieve style points, over and above developing specific accelerated velocities, is woefully being mislead into believing the answers to achieving in the sport of weightlifting are tied to the descriptor of perfect technique alone. Technical precision should be strived for, but perfect technique can never be achieved without achieving certain specific times in motion.

No matter how long one works on trying to develop technical precision, such as the top lifters in the world possess, they will never achieve that level without a continuous increase in performance of certain lifts by using specific accelerated velocities and momentum to achieve those lifts. In other words the top lifters in the world have technical precision, due to the amount of weight they lift and the specific accelerated velocities produced to lift those weights. Having perfect technique alone does not guarantee increases in performance. It takes both technical precision and consistent accelerated velocities to be able to reach those higher levels of performance.

It is far easier to copy or mimic the motion of other top athletes than it is to understand the complexities or physics behind that motion. An athlete cannot learn how to do their event or skill by only being told how to do it in technical terms. They must also be shown how those skills should be executed by the coach or other lifters who are at a high level of proficiency themselves.

Rigid and Ingrain

Rigid or rigidity, may refer to: Stiffness, the property of a solid body to resist deformation, which is sometimes referred to as rigidity.

In the definition of rigid or rigidity, the key is "resist deformation".
Ingrain: Firmly fixed or established; difficult to change.

In the definition of ingrained, the key is "difficult to change".
Efficient, resist deformation and difficult to change are the primers of style or technical efficiency in reference to the athlete's posture, which will be used to produce momentum from acceleration.

My definition of technique, as it refers to any athlete is: Any means necessary within the rules of a sport, that will achieve consistent and constant progress toward the highest accessible level possible.

The Arched Back

In engineering, the arch is one of the strongest structures known because of it's ability to hold back forces through compression. Part of the technique used in weightlifting is the arched back (spine) for both stability and producing greater force and overcoming forces. Good posture is achieved with an arched back which is used to secure the upper torso in an upright and stable position.

Securing erect and rigid posture should not require the athlete to tense their muscles, because posture should be achieved in an effortless and somewhat relaxed position. Inability to arch the lower back is usually a result of inflexibility of the upper back muscles surrounding the scapula. The upper back muscles must be pinched together in order to achieve the arch in the lower back. The back should remain arched throughout any and all lifts. It is most needed during the liftoff, receiving, standing up and during the drive in the jerk and receiving the jerk and standing up with the jerk. Pretty much the whole lift.

Erect and rigid posture is a prerequisite for being able to overcome forces, produce momentum, and increase performance by becoming more stable and therefore more technically precise.

Erect and rigid posture should never change, it should "resist deformation" at all times, during any athletic event. This erect and rigid posture should be achieved in training at all times, and used with each and every lift and or exercise. Absolutely and positively no deviation from this posture should ever occur at any time, either right before, or during a lift. If a lifter deviates posture at any time during a lift it becomes very difficult, actually impossible, for the lifter to be able to ingrain technical precision properly. By the same token, it also becomes more difficult for a lifter to develop inefficient technique and precision of style if correct posture is maintained throughout the lift. The efficiency of technique's focal point should be directed through the arched back, so timing, speed, acceleration, quickness and balance can be stable, and precision of motion can be ingrained to exacting degrees. When catching the weight in the full squat position, in the snatch or clean, the lifter should remain in this erect and rigid posture position for stability, as the legs absorb the shock of catching, securing and standing up with the weight without any balance checks or pauses. As the lifter stands up out of the clean, before the jerk, this erect and rigid posture should be maintained so they don't have to waste time reseting it for the jerk. Resetting posture for the jerk causes a loss in energy that could be used for the jerk; lost energy cannot be regained.

Erect and rigid posture can be characterized as; the back arched, the chest held up and stable, and shoulders held square with the bar, as well as, keeping the head and eyes forward looking throughout the lift. The lifter should avoid extreme motions of the head moving back or down, unless those actions create a more efficient motion for the lifter. The lifter should maintain this erect and rigid posture, during the entire lift, until the head judge gives the down signal.

Erect and rigid posture is never a constant. Even the slightest and almost imperceptible changes in posture can cause a lift to be missed, or executed with less efficiency, causing more energy reserves to be used up in order to complete the lift. Maintaining good posture with the arched back, throughout any lift or exercise, is essential, and should be concentrated on until that motion is ingrained. Posture instabilities can also dissipate the accelerated velocity and therefore the momentum is reduced.

Ingraining Technique

Generally there are three stages an athlete goes through in the beginning process of their career after they have chosen their sport: 1) The athlete, with the aid of a coach, or on their own volition, learns the basic mechanics of that sport 2) The athlete begins to adopt and ingrain those basic motions which will be carried forth during their career. 3) The athlete then begins to develop technical precision and consistent velocities, and this third stage is an ongoing proposition throughout the athlete's career.

Team sports require a variety of various motions which need to be developed, and the athlete should become proficient in all those motions to become a high quality professional athlete. Those skills require many hours of training, to allow the athlete engaged in a team sport, to reach the pinnacle of excellence. Individual sports, such as swimming, speed skating, track and field, and other timed or measured events, as well as weightlifting, contain specific events which are composed of specific motions, and therefore take much less time to learn than it does for a baseball player to learn all their skill-sets. The snatch and clean & jerk can sometimes be quicker to learn than trying to master a variety of less complex motions that are inherently instinctive, such as running, throwing and jumping and even swimming.

Learning the basics of most individual sports does not take very long, and for sports which require fewer motions, the process might only take a few training sessions. Simply learning how to go through a particular motion in a few sessions, such as learning how to snatch or clean & jerk, does not in itself mean the lifter is ready to start piling on the weight to see how much they can lift. Coaches would be remiss in believing they are adept at teaching both the technical skills of an event, and also the skills to lift maximum weights at the same time. Learning a skill might take only a few teaching sessions, but it takes months and even up to a year to gradually develop a foundation before attempting maximum loads. A beginner, regardless of age and regardless of prior abilities for squatting or dead lifting large amounts of weight, should be brought up gradually after learning the lifts, including the squats and pulls.

It should be noted that with the beginning lifter, regardless of age, the only way to ensure the most proficient technique is ingrained, that technique must come from the handling of light weights, or with just enough resistance to learn those skills. If the beginner starts trying to establish PRs too soon, before becoming proficient and precise in their motions, they can ingrain improper motions.

Note: The most common improper motion ingrained by beginners is the act of riding the weight down after receiving it instead of learning how to catch the weight at the lowest possible trajectory point. (This does not include the lighter incremental warmup weights where this type of mechanics is often used).

As the lifter advances the incremental weight, both the precision of each rep, and a specific accelerated velocity must remain constant as the weight increases. Once the lifter can achieve maximum efforts without form or posture breakdowns, without any deceleration during the lift and without riding the weight down after the catch, they are ready to start training their technical precision and velocity.

Developing Precision

Developing precise mechanics of motion into an athlete's technical skill is what creates technical precision of style. Precision of style is what must be developed, and then maintained throughout an athlete's career, which is an ongoing battle, from their first day and until the day they stop competing.

Precision is perfection of motion and velocity repeated in each lift, and in each and every rep regardless of the number of sets or reps or the amount of weight loaded on the bar. Maintaining precision of style, posture and specific velocities requires the lifter to only handle weights that are rarely missed, and can be executed with the lifter's exact same body mechanics of motion from the first rep to the last. There should be only a small amount of deviation in the overall time in motion of the lift or the lifter's established trajectory from one rep to the next.

It is not possible to develop or maintain precision of motion by trying to force precise mechanics by using weights which are too heavy, and cause the lifter to lose that precision, even if they make the lift. Precision of motion cannot be ingrained unless it is constant or never changing.

Any deviations in precision, no matter how imperceptible, will not allow the lifter to reach their full potential. Erratic lifting can cause deviations in motion to occur from one rep to another. It cannot be stressed enough how important it is for the weightlifter to maintain precision of motion and velocity with each and every lift executed in training, and not allow their technique to become erratic, or breakdown for any reason whatsoever. If fatigue sets in causing a decay in the time in motion or erratic lifting to occur, the weight should be reduced enough to complete the number of sets and reps. The lifter should not keep trying to make a lift that was executed improperly, regardless of the cause of that improperly executed lift. The weight should be reduced to where the lift can be executed properly, and then the weight can be advanced if precision can be maintained from that point on.

Lifting with precision is not exactly the same as executing a lift with so called perfect technique, unless that perfect technique is executed each and every time the exact same way. Precision lifting has more to do with how precise the lifter can control their body mechanics, and not allow the weight to control those mechanics during the entire lift, regardless of how much weight is handled or the number of reps being executed.

If the lifter cannot maintain precise motions, through their own particular style and posture, except when using only the bar, they should only use the bar until they can proceed further. With each and every incremental increase in weight, those precise motions must be maintained. Absolutely no deviations in style or posture should ever occur, and posture should never breakdown. Erratic motions must be eliminated for the lifter to ever be able to advance to the highest levels in the sport. In order to progress a motion to it's full potential, that motion has to be precise and the accelerated velocity must be consistent.

Precision training is far more important than setting PRs in the gym using erratic or unstable methods to secure those PRs. Training with precision must become the main priority in the gym over and above setting PRs, unless those PRs can be established with precision and with specific velocity.

It is to be expected, when lifter's approach weights very near, or especially past their PRs, they will possibly experience form breakdowns or erratic motions within their style. Ingraining precision, and maintaining that precision, into the lifter's own particular style and posture, should make it easier to execute lifts properly when they approach near or past their PRs, and even on occasions when the lifter is somewhat fatigued during attempts at certain lifts.

Concentration is not just the ability to ignore certain distractions in the gym while executing a lift. Concentration encompasses the ability of the lifter to focus 100% on each lift and give 100% effort to each lift regardless of how much weight is loaded on the bar, and that concentration must be focused directly at their precision and times in motion, regardless of outside distractions.

Form breakdowns, occurring with weights the lifter is usually able to handle with precision, is a sure sign the lifter is somewhat overtrained, or there is some fatigue in certain parts of the muscular system for a particular lift to be executed without precision. A lack of concentration or taking the weight for granted can be caused by outside stress or overreaching in previous workouts or simply not paying attention to precision and/or velocity requirements.

The younger the lifter, the quicker they will be able to learn and ingrain their style and posture. Once a lifter, of any age, has ingrained their style and posture they will be able to change certain micro-elements within their style, in order to increase their proficiency. The ability to change one's overall style becomes more difficult as time goes by, but small micro changes are not that difficult. Those changes, however, must also be ingrained once adopted.

If erect and rigid posture is not practiced and ingrained from the onset, the lifter's ability to maintain good posture with near maximal weights will become a conscious effort. Any conscious efforts by a lifter can slow down their reaction time during a lift. These conscious efforts are more evident when the lifter becomes accustomed to being told what to do right before they begin a lift. These "shout-outs" or commands by the lifter's coach or training partners can become a crutch to the lifter, and in time, it can become more difficult for the lifter to execute a lift using their own unconscious efforts. Shout-outs and cues should be eliminated as voiced directives. Cues should be executed as an actual physical motion and not as a mental reminder. Mental cues, or shoutouts, can slow down reaction time because the lifter has to think about those cues instead of the lift. The only type of cues a lifter needs are motion cues, like those which will remind them to pull to full extension as quickly as possible or keep the arms straight and relaxed.

The sole purpose of ingraining and maintaining precision is to affect maximum control over the lifter's mechanics of motion, and be able to increase performance through precision and consistent times in motion.

Inertia

Momentum is "mass in motion"
Momentum = mass • velocity

Acceleration is a change in velocity over time.
Inertia refers to an object's amount of resistance to change in velocity, which is quantified by it's mass, or sometimes to its momentum.

Acceleration should be smooth and continuous from the platform to full extension. Any jerking motions or banging the body into the bar can cause that acceleration, and/or the trajectory to be disrupted. Banging into the bar to such an extreme, which causes the bar to oscillate in a non vertical motion, can cause both a change in the trajectory and a loss of momentum and inertia. A less efficient motion will always create an erratic or non-precise motion.

Maximum momentum is achieved as full extension is reached and pulling under the weight is immediately commenced at full extension, so the weight is moving upward while the lifter is moving downward for the catch. If there is any hesitation in pulling under the weight from full extension the momentum will run out sooner before the lifter is able to secure the weight, and the barbell will be accelerating downward and crash on the lifter with greater force than the lifter can control.

"For every action there is an opposite but equal reaction." The accelerated velocity for pulling under the weight is quantified by it's momentum from full extension. Maximum momentum is achieved at full extension and those forces are greatest during maximal ankle flex, and from there that momentum begins to decelerate. The weight fully decelerates at the top of the trajectory. The hang time of the barbell at the top of the trajectory depends on the momentum created from full extension. The barbell carries zero mass for only a micro second, but enough time to get under it so the weight does not drop on the lifter with too much downward velocity.

Weightlifting technique can be characterized as the least amount of momentum needed to lift the maximum amount of weight. The lift or pull from the platform to full extension should be viewed as one motion. Full extension is what allows the lifter to pull under the weight using the lowest trajectory point feasible. Full extension includes the ankle flex, but not the shoulder shrug or arm bending, however, the shoulder shrug does come into play as a gathering of force motion as the lifter is laying back at full extension to begin pulling under the weight.

The farther back the lifter has to lean back, at full extension, the slower the weight was pulled during the 1st pull. This is cause and effect and cannot be changed without otherwise reducing the amount of weight or overcoming those forces during the 1st pull.

Bidirectional and Unidirectional Motions

Specific motions inherent in the events in weightlifting can be described as being bidirectional or unidirectional. This is also true for all other sports, but in a different configuration.

Unidirectional Motions
1) The first pull (from a static start)
2) Standing up with the weight (from a dead stop)
3) Recovering the Jerk

Bidirectional Motions
1) The first pull (from a dynamic start)
2) The transition from the 1st pull to 2nd pull
3) Pulling under the weight or 3rd pull
4) Receiving the snatch or clean
5) Timed rebound (snatch and clean)
6) The dip and drive in the jerk
7) Receiving the jerk

The 1st pull is unidirectional from a static start, because there are no changes in direction from the platform to about mid thigh. The barbell might be pulled inward toward the lifter from the platform to the knees, but that is also a unidirectional motion, since there is no change in direction, i.e., the lifter thrusting the knees forward under the bar. The angular motion might be different from the platform to the knees, but that change does not produce momentum until the bar gets to mid thigh. The gathering of forces or stretch reflex contraction, when raising and lowering the hips into the bar right before liftoff, is a bidirectional motion.

The recovery from the snatch, clean and jerk, not including the timed rebound in the snatch and clean, and full squat jerk, is also unidirectional, or a single motion when standing up out of the snatch or clean or when recovering the jerk from a dead stop. The dip and drive, during the jerk, are bidirectional due to that change in direction.

The unidirectional motions are functions contained in the controlled downward motion in the squats. The recovery is aided by the front squat and the back squat, and the dip is also aided by the controlled downward motion of the front or back squat. The 1st and 2nd pulls are aided by the snatch and clean pull, and the squats also. Controlled does not mean slow, but it does mean the lifter has maximal control over their actions and can redirect those controlled actions into maximal momentum. Controlled actions are more beneficial when they are efficiently and precisely executed at maximal velocity.

The transition from the 1st to the 2nd pull is bidirectional when the knees are pushed forward, in order to pull the weight to full extension which leads to another change in direction; the 3rd pull.

Pulling under the weight is a transitional phase between the 2nd to 3rd pull where the change in direction is from an upward motion to a downward motion immediately at the point full extension (apex) is reached. Receiving the weight in the snatch, clean and the jerk are bidirectional due to the changes in direction.

The timed rebound, when used in the snatch and clean, is bidirectional due to the downward and immediate upward motion from the bounce out of the full squat position, i.e., a rapid change in direction. Even during a power snatch or clean there still should be a rapid change in direction.

The dip and drive in the jerk is bidirectional due to the transitional phase between the dip and the jerk drive, creating a change in direction. Receiving the weight at the top of the trajectory is a change in direction of the lifter from full extension to a downward direction for receiving the weight.

Unidirectional motions are used to overcome forces, not to produce momentum, and bidirectional motions are used to increase accelerated velocity and produce inertia from momentum. During unidirectional motions forces have to be overcome or controlled, and bidirectional motions generate force or momentum. The more control (overcoming force) the lifter has over those unidirectional motions the more optimum force they can generate during the bidirectional motions. Action reaction based motions occur at the point of no return, i.e., where the lifter is forced to drive the knees forward or forced to pull under the weight, simply because they have already committed themselves to those actions. Those actions go a long way in determining how the squats and pulls should be executed with respect to precision and specific times in motion.

The point where maximum momentum is achieved is at full extension, so at any time before that maximum amount of momentum can be produced, it is the lifter that is moving and the barbell is following along with the lifter's motions. The lifter is overcoming forces during the 1st pull, and that changes to producing forces during the 2nd pull to full extension. This concept should be fully understood to recognize the duality of purpose of the pulls and squats, and to understand why the pulls and squats should, for the vast majority of training, be executed with specific times in motion or constant velocities, regardless of the weight on the bar. These times in motion need to match up with both the bidirectional and unidirectional motions achieved during the snatch and clean & jerk. Also, they must match up with the specific overall times in motion of the snatch and clean from the platform to standing up with the weight. The amount of weight handled in the squats and pulls should be limited to what the lifter can achieve at those specific and consistent times in motion.

The intricate transitional phases that occur between the 1st, 2nd and 3rd pull, and the dip and drive of the jerk are difficult to develop in parts. These transitions are left out when attempting to do parts of a pull, and that alone can disrupt the flow of the acceleration and changes in direction. Now parts of the pull can be executed, but only with enough weight that will allow for those transitional phases to stay in agreement with the transitional phases of the full movements, through exact positioning, for example, doing cleans without jerks and jerks without cleans leaves out the transitional phase between the clean and the jerk.

The beginning lifter can be taught how to lift in parts, and might become somewhat proficient at doing those parts, but it is the full movement that determines how proficient the lifter will become. The beginner should never use parts of a lift to advance their skills, but only advance those skills by doing the full movements. Lifting off boxes and using straps should be postponed as long as possible or until the lifter reaches a point where they need the straps and can achieve the same position when lifting off boxes as when lifting off the platform, and neither the use of straps or boxes have any adverse effect on the lifter reaching their full potential. Any PR snatch achieved with straps off the platform should not be considered a PR and the lifter should be aware that they might not be able to do the same amount in competition without those straps. Straps should never be used in the clean & jerk for safety concerns during the jerk. Straps will also allow more weight to be cleaned than is necessary or beneficial for the lifter to progress.

As the bar travels from the platform to mid thigh, or where the knees are pushed forward, overcoming forces shifts to generating force. These forces, if not overcome, can create drag, and the 1st pull can feel like a heavy dead lift at times. In order to reduce drag, the lifter should be able to pull from the platform to mid thigh in it at least .5 seconds for optimum velocity. The accelerated velocity should be continuous and transitioned smoothly from the platform to full extension.

The 1st and 2nd pull are linked together, due to the shape of the human body, in a way that causes the change in acceleration from the 1st pull to affect the 2nd pull and visa versa. The 1st pull can be slower than .5 seconds, but that will effect the 2nd pull's force production and the amount of weight the lifter is capable of lifting. The time in motion may or may not be affected in the 2nd pull, just the ability to produce greater force at the transitional phase, because the transitional velocity is slower and the 2nd pull action will be less forceful, not necessarily slower, since force is increased through a faster change in acceleration. If the 1st pull is too forceful it could disrupt the production of force during the 2nd pull and the 3rd pull. This is why acceleration has to be smooth and continuous, so there are no disruptions in acceleration during the transitional phases.

The .5 second 1st pull is optimum for reaching high levels in the sport. Slower times in motion will not affect the 2nd pull velocity or the velocity of the 3rd pull, it will just not allow as much weight to be lifted as could be lifted with the .5 second 1st pull. In other words the amount of weight lifted is tied to specific times in motion and the forces that can be overcome to generate those specific times. It has less to do with how much weight can be squatted or dead lifted without regard to those specific times or force production capabilities. In fact, slow grinding squats and dead lifts actually reduce the lifters ability to overcome or generate more force and specific times in motion needed for optimum efficiency during the snatch and clean & jerk.

The angle in the back during the initial pull off the platform should be somewhat fixed, but can change when the bar is just in front of the knees or above the knees, or for some lifters even below the knees. The back should not be forced or caused to rotate downward during the 1st pull. This is a sign the lifter has less stability in the lower back or the back is not fully arched, to be able to keep it from rotating downward thereby covering the bar more than is necessary. There might also be some issue with the correct velocity to overcome those forces that cause too much drag on the lifter to keep from rotating the back downward. The downward rotation during the 1st pull creates a slower time in motion from the platform to the 2nd pull position. It also disrupts the acceleration and consequently the 2nd pull will be less forceful.

The knees move forward when the bar is around mid thigh or a little lower. The position of the bar depends on the lifter's proportions and/or their particular style of lifting. Producing acceleration must be developed through the sensitivity of the lifter, during these transitional phases, not necessarily by what the coach sees. The perceptions of an outside observer can be deceiving even to a coach's eye, but are less deceiving to the person engaged in performing a bidirectional motion where momentum is being produced. Coaches should not dictate positions for lifters, unless the coach knows for sure those positions will make the lifter more proficient. Experimentation is the key to finding the right solution.

The 1st pull takes the barbell from the platform to around mid thigh. The shins are moved back to allow the bar to pass the knees, and the knees stay back until the bar reaches around mid thigh, where the 2nd pull is to begin. One variation of the snatch and clean pull is to lift the weight up to just where the 2nd pull is to be commenced, but the action is stopped at that point and the barbell is let back down from there to the platform. The knees should be pushed back as far as possible during the transition from the knees to mid thigh or even allow the bar to be pulled in toward the lap, but still keeping the knees back in a vertical position.

It is very important for lifters to understand the 1st pull is from the platform to mid thigh in both the snatch and clean and not just to the knees. It is also important to realize the positions called 1st, 2nd and 3rd pull are transitional and are not static positions. It is impossible to just practice the 3rd pull and just as impossible to practice doing a 2nd pull or 1st pull without those transitional phases. Yes, the 1st and 2nd pull can be executed as separate motions, but those separate motions will never be the exact same as when doing the full movement.

Note: I use the word pull, because that word has been around the sport for ages. In actuality, there should be no pulling in weightlifting during a lift, except when pulling under the weight. The lifter is simply using their legs, hips and upper torso to lift the weight into a favorable position to extract maximum momentum through their own body mechanics of motion, as the lifter is accelerating upward. The arms are used simply to hold onto the weight during the lift from the platform to full extension. The arms should stay relaxed before the lift-off, and not overly tensed or bent until the 3rd pull begins. This requires a strong enough grip on the bar to allow the lifter to keep the arms somewhat relaxed and straight throughout the 1st and 2nd pull.

The 2nd pull is the shortest of the three pulling phases. Once the bar reaches about mid thigh the lifter only needs to fully extend the body in a somewhat laid back position using the ankle flex and keeping the arms straight towards full extension.

The arms should be as straight as possible through full extension. There is no such thing as a power position as far as it being a static point with a specific purpose. Any attempt at trying to force the feet to stay flat until the upper torso is vertical will more than likely create a less than stellar performance. During the snatch the ankle flex is more often than not commenced before the so called power position is reached. During the clean the feet tend to stay flat footed when the upper torso is vertical, but is not always such. The human body is diverse in its skeletal proportions and muscular densities throughout the body, and might compel the lifter to achieve certain positions which might not be considered the norm with respect to the intellectual's perspective. Such as, the knees moving inward during parts of the lift or the arms bending during parts of the 1st or 2nd pull. Almost any type of so called imperfect technique can be seen in even the world's best lifters, especially during world record attempts. The key to lifting is precision of motion with a consistent velocity, not simply perfection of technique.

Immediately upon pulling under the weight the feet should be repositioned back down on the platform as quickly as possible to form a stable base from which to receive the barbell. Remember, at the point of full extension the maximal amount of momentum has already been placed into the weight to allow the lifter to pull under it as quickly as possible. The feet or ankle flex is used to direct the action of pulling under the weight, not for producing momentum, likewise, the shoulder shrug is used to pull under the weight by using a small amount of shoulder rotation and pinching the muscles in the upper back together to stabilize the arch in the back for receiving the weight.

In order to pull under the weight, using the maximal momentum from the 2nd pull, the feet can be moved outward laterally as fast as possible and as far as possible.

Any extension of the toes vertically, for too long a period of time, will cause the lifter to float at the top of full extension, even if the feet are moved laterally after the toe raise. The ankle extension should be simultaneous with a lateral motion of the feet. This action if done correctly will force the lifter into a downward motion almost automatically. The lateral foot movement is an action/reaction based motion, where going high on the toes vertically is cause and effect. The prolonged high toe raise affects the momentum the barbell achieves before being able to pull under it, sooner, quicker and lower. A prolonged high ankle flex can also cause the lifter to bend the arms prematurely before pulling under the weight, which is also cause and effect.

Reaction time is critical for pulling under the weight as the lifter is rotating the upper torso from a vertical position to a laid back position. There can be no hesitation for even a split second in transitioning from full extension to pulling under the weight. Once the lifter's torso is vertical and the feet are still flat on the platform it is near impossible to cut the pull short or not go to full extension, but it is possible to over pull the weight. The lifter must be trained properly on how to pull into the full squat position so the weight does not drop down on the lifter with more force than they can control, and not over pull the weight and ride the lift down into the full squat position or worse, reach the full squat position with the weight fully accelerating downward at the same time.

The Gathering of Forces (Elastic Recoil)

The "gathering of forces" is the action a weightlifter takes, in order to ready themselves to initiate the pull off the platform. The mechanics of motion during the gathering of forces phase are different from sport to sport, but the motion after the gathering of forces phase is generally the same principle of producing momentum through the legs, hips and upper torso by using particular changes in direction.

All sporting events require an athlete to gather their forces, due to the purpose of action, and this gathering of forces is for one reason and one reason only: to ready the athlete to transfer the greatest amount of momentum into the initiation of that action. The extension of the body is the culminating action of their event, and causes a reaction, which if done with the most efficient speed, timing, balance and control, should result in the best performance the athlete can achieve on that day, with the effective strength (velocity) they have available and through their own precise body mechanics of motion through the use of the legs, hips and upper torso.

Initiating action is achieved by raising and lowering the hips into the bar. This stretch-shortening cycle increases the force of contraction on the initial liftoff. A static liftoff will not deliver as much initial force as a dynamic liftoff. However, the gathering of forces is more timing intense the more dynamic it is. For the purposes of weightlifting, only a small amount of motion is needed before liftoff, and some lifters use such a small gathering of force phase it is almost undetectable, however, it is close to impossible to actually begin the pull with a pure static start, because some contraction is necessary the split second before liftoff in order to activate the muscles needed for that liftoff.

There are two gathering of forces phases in the snatch and four in the clean & jerk. The initial liftoff in both the snatch and clean & jerk, right before the timed rebound in both the snatch and clean & jerk, right before the dip in the jerk and right before the drive in the jerk.

Accelerated velocity must be generated in a smooth and continuous motion for it to be efficiently applied and controlled. Any jerking motions, such as banging the hips or thighs into the bar, can cause irregular trajectories at any phase of the lift, and that can dampen the momentum. This would also include the gathering of forces phase before the 1st pull, where the lifter might accidentally scrape the bar against the shins or knee(s). Even a very slight grazing of the chin during the jerk will kill the momentum and change the trajectory and the jerk cannot be completed. Changes in acceleration are a delicate matter and it takes very little to throw that acceleration off. Attempts at being so called explosive during the 2nd pull should not be taken to mean the production of a jerky motion using the hips.

Section 2: The Elements of Technique

Technique does not include style variations. Technique is purely a concern between the efficiency of motion and the expenditure of energy between the legs, hips and upper torso. The rules, for example, do not expressly disallow any particular grip spacing for either the snatch or clean or jerk. Style variations do not impact the technical elements, but can have an impact on the amount of weight that could be lifted.

There should be no difference in technique, with respect to the 1st and 2nd pull, between a high snatch or full snatch, both should be executed exactly the same. There should also be no difference in technique between a clean grip snatch and regular snatch. What some view as technical elements are in most cases only variations in style, but should have no impact on the major lifting elements which make up technique and are the same for all lifters. I would be very leery of those who give pet names to particular motions and claim there is something different about the way they do those motions, when they cannot define that difference. For example, the freestyle event in competitive swimming is executed almost exactly the same way by all the top level swimmers in the world. The top level thrower's technique in track & field are almost mirror images of each other, especially in the discus or hammer throw, at least with respect to the actions surrounding the legs, hips and upper torso.

Style or Form Variations

The sport of weightlifting requires certain elements, contained in the mechanics of motion of that sport, to be adhered to strictly in order for the athlete to perform those events with optimum efficiency. Athletes have many and various characteristics which can go a long way in dictating their particular style. There are also variations in the style an athlete can use to make them feel more comfortable, or more efficient during their performance.

1) Foot placement
2) Hand spacing
3) Hip position
4) The type of style used in the jerk
5) The arched back
6) The release of the hook grip

How close together or far apart the feet are placed under the bar to begin the pull, or the jerk, is a personal preference of the lifter and something that makes the lifter feel more efficient, but has little bearing on the basic fundamental mechanics of motion of either the snatch or clean & jerk. Some lifters use what is called a frog style, where the heels are positioned closer than the toes, and in some cases the heels are together. Some lifters keep their feet in a straight line, and space them in many various distances apart. The frog style can also be used to move the thighs outward during the pull, thereby allowing the lifter to keep the bar in closer to their body during the 1st pull.

The spacing of the hands on the bar is also a personal preference for the lifter. There are numerous reasons lifters choose a particular hand spacing, but for the most part that adaptation of style is geared toward finding the most advantageous width that can be used to increase the lifter's proficiency. This particular adaptation is probably the most experimented with in all of lifting. Generally the hand spacing becomes a fixed component, and is never altered throughout a lifter's career. A less efficient hand spacing might keep the lifer from lifting up to their capabilities, but has no bearing on the actual technique of the lift. The arms and hands are only used to hold onto the bar as the lifter uses their legs, hips and upper torso to lift the weight off the platform and produce the necessary momentum. If the arms are kept straight and relaxed during the pull to full extension more momentum can be produced than if the arms are used as a mechanical advantage (bent), although that could be a mechanical disadvantage.

The moving of the feet laterally, in order to receive the weight, is an important style variation for receiving the weight at the lowest possible trajectory point. Top lifters do not always move the feet outward, and some don't move them at all, other than a slight toe raise, but the lateral motion does allow the lifter to pull under the weight quicker and somewhat lower. There are many variations as far as the use of the feet are concerned, but there is no one variation that can be said to be perfect for everyone.

How high or low a lifter's hips are stationed at the beginning of a pull is often times dictated by theories or philosophies from lifters or coaches. The hips, however, are not in question, it's the angle of the thigh and back that are in question. The hips will follow the extension of the legs during the 1st pull and the back will follow the initial angle of the legs if the back is fixed in position during the 1st pull. During the snatch, if the thighs are parallel to the platform or a bit below parallel at liftoff and only the legs are used to lift the weight up to the knees, by keeping the back in a fixed position, the hips will follow that action. This is the preferred style used in the snatch. If only the legs are used to lift the weight up to the knees then the lifter can stay wedged into the bar longer and keep the bar in closer to the body through full extension. This same style should also be used in the clean, but the angle of the thighs is greater at liftoff, due to a narrower grip.

If the legs are opened up too soon at liftoff then more of the back muscles must be used to lift the weight, and the back is not as strong as the legs are. The back has to be developed enough to overcome the forces at liftoff to maintain the fixed angle while the legs do most of the work getting the bar to the area of the 2nd pull. If the back is forced downward during the 1st pull the hips will rise up and cause the back muscles to come into play too soon and create some fatigue or loss of contraction during the 2nd pull. Even so, the positioning of the hips at liftoff is mostly a style variation, and might effect the lifter's ability to lift more weight, but it has nothing to do with the major technical elements of lifting, which must be used by everyone or the rules would have to be altered to cover all applications.

The rules do not expressly state the knees have to resend during the 2nd pull; the rules only express that the weight must be lifted from the platform overhead in the snatch and to the shoulders in the clean using one continuous motion.

A particular style used by the lifter to execute their jerk is also a preference, and has little bearing on how much more weight can be jerked. Using one style over another, such as the split, so called power jerk, or full squat jerk is a personal choice. Strength (force) and specific velocities must be developed into whatever style the lifter chooses to use for their jerk.

The arched back is a necessary element, but some lifters cannot arch the back at liftoff. In this case the back should remain rigid in whatever position they can achieve, but even that is not always possible.

Letting go of the hook grip when receiving the weight in the snatch and clean, and receiving the bar on the fingertips, has more to do with flexibility of the lifter in the shoulder area, and/or upper back. This would be a style element due to necessity. Most lifters let go of the hook grip before the jerk. Keeping the hook grip in the snatch and clean can create more stability in receiving the weight, but this is not always possible or necessarily preferred.

Style variations may aid the lifter, but the lifter would lift just about the same amount of weight no matter what variations they adopted. This is in large part due to the fact that in the final analysis it is the amount of force the lifter can overcome and produce, which has been developed through the squats and pulls, that determines how much weight can be lifted, not necessarily through any particular style variation.

In some cases, a lifter might adopt a style variant which could become antagonistic to their ability to progress, without knowing it. This is why it is very important to experiment with all the different elements to make sure the most beneficial elements are adopted.

Just about anyone off the street can reach down and grab the bar and lift it up, at least to a standing position, as long as they have the strength. But without certain skills the ordinary person is incapable of hoisting a maximum effort weight over their head by squatting downward to catch it. This is because they lack either the nerve or knowledge to squat down under a weight they have lifted up off the ground overhead. This takes specific and strict mechanics of motion inherent only in the sport of weightlifting, and not seen or used in everyday life or in other sports.

Technical Elements

In order to get to the actual basic technical elements of weightlifting then style variations have to be discarded as part of that discussion. The technical rules state that in the snatch the weight must be lifted off the platform to arms length in one continuous motion without any re-bending of the elbows or pressing out motions. There are no rules with respect to how the legs, hips and upper torso should move, other than the knees or butt cannot touch the platform during the lift or the elbows touch the thighs. What is left are technical elements that are a concern of accelerated velocity, and that is where the motions and style variations are derived. The faster the athlete moves, the more precise their motions will have to be in order to become proficient enough to continue to advance their skills to their full potential.

The following key elements in weightlifting should be achieved when executing a snatch or clean & jerk in order to apply the lifter's style variations efficiently, and be able to achieve their best performance with technical precision and optimum momentum from specific changes in acceleration.

1) Snatch and Clean & Jerk
   a) From the platform to full extension (1st and 2nd pull) the accelerated velocity should be controlled, smooth and continuous.
   b) The third pull should take half the time as the pull to full extension.
   c) The weight should be received at the lowest trajectory point necessary with the upper torso in a vertical position when receiving the weight.

2) The Jerk
   a) The dip should be smooth, controlled and vertical.
   b) The drive should be faster than the dip and the push under the weight should be faster than the drive.
   c) The weight should be received at the lowest trajectory point necessary and the upper torso should be vertical upon receiving the weight.

The most important phase or element of lifting occurs at the beginning of the lift, where the weight is pulled from the platform to the 2nd pull position. This must be accomplished using quick reaction time, and controlled acceleration, so unnecessary additional forces are not placed on the body which might adversely affect the 2nd pull. The ability to overcome forces created during the 1st pull can be achieved by some overloading in the pulls and squats through specific times in motion which are in agreement with the 1st pull velocity. Overloading does not exclude specific velocities; it must include them regardless of the amount of weight loaded on the bar, i.e., the weight should not decelerate.

Deceleration means the weight slows down at some point between the liftoff the platform and the 2nd pull transitional position. Deceleration is sometimes called grinding out the lift, and this should be avoided at all costs. The weight can move at the same velocity, but should never, once started off the platform, move slower at any particular position.

The time from the platform to full extension is about .67 seconds for the snatch and clean. It becomes almost irrelevant how the lifter reaches the fully extended position if these times in motion are achieved. Due to the shape of the human body and the laws of physics all lifters lift the weight from the platform to full extension in the same general motion. After that is where things separate the top world lifters from all others. Which is their ability to pull under the weight very quickly and receive the weight at the lowest trajectory point possible, even by spreading the feet out farther than is normally necessary. The top lifters posses exceptional timing during their changes in direction to where the greatest amount of momentum is achieved through the elimination of all unnecessary motions or including motions that make it possible to achieve their maximal weights. They possess uncanny degrees of mobility, flexibility and speed to attack the weight using whatever motion(s) it takes to make the lift, even if their actions seem to be somewhat chaotic.

Note: The idea there is such a thing as a Russian, Bulgarian or Chinese pull is an irrational concept. Unless these lifters came from another planet it is my understanding that human beings are all made the same way, yet even Russians have different body types so it is absurd to think that even all Russians pull the exact same way. Even if this were true it makes no difference since the pull to full extension should be .67 seconds regardless of how the weight is pulled.

It is important to learn how to lift so the 1st and 2nd pull feels as one motion from the platform to full extension and learn to transfer that momentum into the pull under the weight where the weight can be caught at the lowest possible trajectory point achievable for each individual lifter.

The Three Phases of the Pull

The three pulling phases are basically a breakdown of the changes in direction, based on the structure of the human body with regard to lifting an object with the intent to create enough inertia from momentum to squat under the weight to receive it, before the weight begins to move in a downward direction.

Phase 1: From the platform to around mid thigh or where the 2nd pull begins or at the point the hips are driven forward.

Generally, lifters use either a static start position or an elastic contraction (gathering of forces) before liftoff. The position of the hips is also varied and depends on the lifter's body proportions, as well as their ratio of squat to pull. The main criterion is what is most efficient for the lifter, in order to overcome the forces applied to the body during the 1st pull, and produce enough of a smooth controlled change in acceleration to produce maximal momentum during the 2nd pull, and maintain their position or back angle.

Phase 2: From where the hips are driven forward and then toward full extension.

There is no such thing as a double knee bend. The knees unbend at liftoff and then re-bend when the 2nd pull is commenced. The bending of the knees right before liftoff does not count as a double knee bend since the weight has not left the platform.

Note: The misleading word "explode" is used rather often in many sports. The thought of exploding has a rather dubious connotation to it. But suffice it to say no athlete can or does explode at any time during an event. Again, acceleration should be smooth and continuous and changes in direction should be achieved as quickly as possible, but in no way should an athlete explode during a 2nd pull. The thought explode could cause the lifter to yank or jerk on the weight at the wrong timing point.

Phase 3: Pulling under the weight in order to receive it at the lowest possible trajectory point.

Phase 2 and phase 3 are transitional at the point where the lifter's head is at the top of the apex, between full extension and pulling under the weight. The lateral movement of the feet should commence quickly as the lifter begins pulling under the weight. Once the back goes past vertical, the transition from the 2nd pull to pulling under the weight should begin immediately to allow the momentum to carry the weight upward while the lifter is moving downward.

There should be some slight bend in the legs at full extension when this transition is executed. The arms are kept straight even as the lifter is laying back. From that laid back position the change in direction must be very quick and controlled. The arms are only bent enough to pull under the weight and rotate the elbows forward very quickly in the clean. The elbows are not rotated forward in the snatch, but are locked out overhead vertically from a rotational motion of the wrists.

The only purpose of bending the arms and shrugging the shoulders is to pull under the weight, however, the shoulders are shrugged as the lifter is laying back. The spreading of the feet outward is also a condition of the transitional phase initiated as the upper torso goes past vertical, in order to transfer that momentum to pulling under the weight to receive it. The feet must be quickly spread apart, and quickly arrive back down on the platform, or if the feet are not spread apart, the ankle flex must be achieved by going slightly up on the toes and coming back down quickly to a flatfooted position. The longer the lifter is up on their toes, the longer it takes to pull under the weight (cause and effect; referred to as floating).

The lifter's head should actually swing in an arc type motion and not an up and down motion. The arch is more pronounced in the snatch than the clean. As the lifter reaches a full laid back position, the weight is moving upward from the momentum from phase 1 and 2, not from phase 3. Full momentum must be achieved at the end of phase 2, before pulling under the weight. Maximal momentum is used to transition from the 2nd pull into the 3rd pull.

Again the slower the 1st pull is (slower than .5 seconds) the farther the laid back position will be. This keeps the lifter from handling more weight, but since they have less ability to overcome initial forces off the platform it allows them to handle weights they could not handle otherwise, and especially if they catch the weight at a very low trajectory point.

Full momentum is reached at full extension with some small assistance from the ankle extension in conjunction with the velocity created by the legs, hips and upper torso. This momentum from the legs, hips and upper torso actually causes the ankle extension, because it is near impossible to stay flatfooted when snatching or cleaning a weight over 85% of PR. The ankle extension is action/reaction based or an involuntary action.

As the lifter begins pulling under the weight, the feet are quickly returned to the platform, and the upper torso is whipped forward to a vertical position as quickly as possible to receive the weight in an upright position. The weight is captured and secured at the full squat position in the snatch and at the parallel position in the clean. The lifter rides the weight down into the full squat from parallel in the clean in order to achieve a timed rebound. The downward motion from parallel to full is the gathering of forces phase used to achieve the timed rebound. If the lifter catches the weight in the full squat position in the clean, it will be more difficult to execute a timed rebound and the lifter will have to stand up out of a dead stop or execute a rebound from a paused squat or even a double bounce rebound.

Note: The only difference between a high snatch and clean, and a full squat snatch and clean, is that the momentum necessary for the high snatch or clean carries the barbell higher in order to catch it at the higher position. There should be no fundamental difference in technique, other than that aspect concerning momentum which is controlled by the amount of weight vs. the ability of the lifter to produce the right momentum to receive a high snatch or clean.

The ankle flex, or toe raise and shoulder shrug, should not be executed for the purpose of placing more height on the weight, or it will cause the lifter to drift upward instead of quickly moving downward. Maximum momentum must be produced by the legs, hips and upper torso, and not through the arms, ankles or shoulder shrug. If the lifter stays on the toes too long, and goes too high on the toes in a vertical direction, they will over pull the weight, which adds additional time in motion, and they lose the ability to catch the weight at the lowest possible trajectory point. This is cause and effect, It limits the action/reaction-based momentum to allow for pulling under the weight lower. This in itself does not cause a lift to be missed, but it does cause the lifter to not be able to lift the maximum amount of weight they are capable of. If one wishes to become a top lifter, they cannot be floating up in the air on their toes like a ballerina, or trying to do a vertical jump while holding onto the barbell. The ankle flex and shoulder shrug should only be used to direct the downward motion of the lifter under the weight, as quick and as low as they can go, with the downward motion of the barbell being the least amount before securing the weight.

Note: The problem with doing snatch or clean high pulls with maximal weights is that action teaches the lifter to over pull the weight using the arms after full momentum (extension) has been reached. Snatch or clean high pulls have nothing to do with the 3rd pull. The 3rd pull cannot be simulated when doing pulls. Snatch and clean high pulls should be executed with very light weights or during the warmups using the empty bar.

The downward motion of pulling under the weight (not the initiation of that motion) and upon receiving the weight (not securing the barbell) is neither a unidirectional or bidirectional motion. It is part of the flight or trajectory of the lifter in the opposite direction where there are no forces to produce or overcome, other than those smaller forces associated with the timing, balance and velocity of the downward rotation of the lifter under the bar to receive it. The momentum generated from the 2nd pull will allow the lifter to pull under the weight using the momentum from that 2nd pull to increase the momentum of the 3rd pull. Where the pull from the platform to full extension should be close to .67 seconds, the 3rd pull should be .33 seconds or half the pull to full extension, regardless of it being a full squat snatch or power snatch.

There are few action/reaction based motions when doing the snatch and clean & jerk. The lifter needs to control almost all those action/reaction motions in one way or another, with the exception of the gathering of forces motions, the ankle extension and shoulder shrug. Lifting maximal weights overhead and squatting down to catch those weights is not as natural as running, throwing or jumping. In order to control the action the lifter has to control their precision and accelerated velocity to exacting degrees. When the accelerated velocities breakdown the action/reaction phases might not be completed to where a lift can be executed correctly or even successfully.

Style variations with respect to the feet are numerous. Some lifters like to lift their feet under them and then stomp the feet back down on the platform before receiving the weight. Others wedge the feet back down to the platform toe to heel and quieter. Some spread the feet and some don't, some have the toes leave the platform and others don't. Each lifter has to find the style variation that works best for them. It should be understood that a lot of times these style variations are not always done the exact same way, for any particular lifter, each and every lift, and sometimes that depends on the amount of weight on the bar or how much force has to be overcome, or how little.

Recovery Out of the Snatch and Clean

Once the lifter has secured the weight, they should execute a timed rebound in order to stand up with the weight. The timed rebound is a bidirectional motion preceded by a gathering of forces motion during the time the lifter is securing the weight. The timed rebound is the preferred method and the most athletic type of motion for the snatch or clean recovery. There are two other methods that are also used, a forced timed rebound from a slight pause, and recovery from a dead stop out of the full squat position.

If the lifter comes to a dead stop in the full squat position, the timed rebound cannot be executed, but a forced rebound out of the squat position can be, or the lifter can simply stand up out of a dead stop. Without a rebound the motion becomes a simple unidirectional motion, and it takes longer to stand than a forced rebound, and a forced rebound takes longer to stand than a timed rebound. The timed rebound generates more momentum for the lifter to stand up faster, than the other two methods. The timed rebound should be the primary method used when training the snatch and clean. The muscles used in the timed rebound must be trained enough to achieve this motion smoothly and unconsciously, and ingrain this action so it becomes technically precise and with a consistent velocity (time in motion).

The lifter can stand up out of the squat position by keeping the upper torso vertical or leaning forward through the sticking point, and then coming to a vertical position once the sticking point has been passed. The lifter can lean forward more in recovering a snatch than they can the clean. The preferred method is keeping the upper torso as vertical as possible throughout the lift, through what I call forced mobility.

When using the timed rebound, the thighs will move inward, due to the force placed on the hips during the rebound. The amount the thighs are forced inward can be of varying degrees, and sometimes almost unnoticed. Attempting to force the thighs to stay outward during a heavy clean recovery could be somewhat futile, and could cause the timed rebound to be less efficient. At times the thighs might be forced outward when going through the sticking point. The motion of the thighs moving inward and/or outward is a reflection of how the squats are trained and how the lifter's ability to overcome force is distributed throughout their muscular system, for any particular moment, and especially where accelerated velocities are concerned.

Torque is created from a rotation upon an axis point, such as throwers use in track and field. Moving the knees inward or outward symmetrically, neutralizes rotational torque, and forces a symmetrical or leveraging of motion, or squeezes the lifter upward using the larger muscles in the buttocks. If this torque is not neutralized it can cause the lifter to windmill during the recovery.

The timed rebound, I would consider to be the correct and most efficient mechanics of motion. The timed rebound is easier to achieve in the clean than in the snatch, where balance during a snatch can be a problem at times. Both the clean and snatch should be trained using a timed rebound so standing up can be quick, and as effortless as possible. Learning to lift by sitting in the bottom of a snatch or clean will require more energy to be expended and a slower time in motion when standing up will almost certainly have to be executed.

Another reason to move the feet outward laterally or farther than where the lifter initiated the pull is so the hips can be brought in closer to the bar when receiving the weight, and this can aid in a lower and more stable catch of the weight.

Note: The correct muscles are brought into play due to whatever motion is employed. It is not so easy to define a motion by how the muscular system behaves. There is no way I know of to force the muscular system to behave differently or other than involuntarily or instinctively to a particular motion. To do so would necessitate a conscious effort and that alone would slow down the process of contraction, at least during a bidirectional motion. Force production is developed throughout the muscular system as a whole for the benefit of the competition lifts' bidirectional motions, not for individual muscles, as in bodybuilding. Training the muscles to behave like a bodybuilder's could be antagonistic to the sport of weightlifting and produce negative results.

After the lifter has stood up with the weight in the clean the lifter must be ready to execute the jerk, of which there are also three phases to go through. The gathering of forces occurs right before the dip is commenced.

1) The dip
The dip should be achieved with control, by going down a bit slower than the drive or the same velocity, but never faster than the drive. The upper torso should be perfectly vertical during the dip. The elbows should stay at the same angle from the top of the dip to the lowest point before the drive. The lifter should stay flatfooted with a solid base to begin the drive from. The weight will automatically be distributed to the heels during the dip if the lifter stays perfectly vertical. Dipping downward too fast can cause the

lifter to loose contact with the bar on the shoulders and the bar will crash back down on the lifter at the lowest trajectory of the dip, and right before the drive is commenced. The knees can be flared outward or kept straight forward during the dip and the lifter should decide which style works best for them. Sometimes the lifter should make a conscious effort to raise the elbows and chest right before the dip commences to make sure the elbows are raised to a position that will not cause the lifter to use the arms during the drive.

2) The drive

The drive should commence the split second the lifter has reached the lowest point in the dip. It should be executed with extreme quickness, speed and precision. The drive to full extension should be a very short time in motion, and full momentum is achieved the split second the bar leaves the shoulders. Once the bar leaves the shoulders, no more momentum can be generated. The same principle that applies to reaching full extension in the snatch and clean, as far as generating full momentum is concerned, applies to the drive in the jerk. The depth of the dip is dependent on the amount of momentum that can be produced during the drive. From the lowest trajectory to locking out the arms takes about .5 seconds.

The drive includes the ankle flex and shoulder shrug as a transitional motion as the lifter goes to full extension in the drive and then pushes under the weight to receive it. The arms should never be used during the jerk, snatch or clean. The arms are only there for the lifter to hold onto the bar while the legs, hips and torso do the lifting, and support the weight overhead.

If the feet have been spread outward during the clean and recovery, they can be brought back together close enough to spread them outward again for the jerk. If the feet stay spread out for the split jerk, and the feet come back in a small bit when splitting the feet apart, then this can cause some balance problems. For a stable landing during the split jerk, the feet should be spread outward, as well as, forward and back. The front foot in the split can be turned inward a bit and the back foot can be kept straight forward toward the knee, or can also be turned inward a small amount. Some lifters even turn the back foot outward and this is normally due to a non-symmetrical physiology or a technical mistake, and once the lift is successful neither should be considered wrong.

3) Receiving the weight

Once the bar leaves the shoulders the lifter is either splitting under the weight or squatting under it to receive it. The head is laid back to allow for a vertical trajectory, and as soon as the bar passes the head the upper torso and head are quickly moved forward to allow the bar to become stationed just above the back of the head when the weight is secured. From the drive to locking out the elbows should take .5 seconds, .6 seconds at the most, and .47 seconds for optimum efficiency. The bar should be pushed to the locked out position quickly, and not allow the body to be pushed downward more than is necessary to secure the weight under the rules governing the jerk.

The feet should be split apart enough so the thigh of the front leg is almost parallel to the platform. There can be some bend in the back leg and the amount is dependent on choice. The main thing is the front thigh achieving just above parallel, so the jerk does not become a power split jerk.

There is some margin for error, depending on where the feet come back down in the split style. There is much less margin for error in the power jerk or squat jerk. The lifter is actually pushing themselves under the weight as the bar leaves the shoulders and not afterwards. However, it's the amount of momentum on the weight that allows the lifter to push under it and push it to lockout quicker. The faster the drive, the faster the lifter can push downward under the weight. This is cause and effect because the depth of the dip depends on the drive velocity, i.e., the faster the drive velocity the shorter the dip. The drive from the dip is not action/reaction because the lifter does not have to commence the drive after the dip. The drive must be commenced and controlled by the lifter throughout that particular change in direction.

Generally the feet should come back down at the same time, or at least the forces should be returned to both feet equally. The toe of the back foot might hit the platform before the front foot, but the forces placed on the feet have to be equalized upon receiving the weight. This should become instinctive and not become a conscious effort.

4) Recovering the Jerk
Once the weight is secured overhead, the lifter must stand up with the weight with the feet in line for the down signal. To achieve this the lifter can move the front foot back first and then bring the back foot forward, and then adjust them in line for the down signal, or move the back foot in first and in line with the front foot, or small variations of these

movements. These movements will help keep the lifter under the bar, while the lifter is moving the feet inward, depending on where the bar is overhead. The recovery in the split is not time dependent, but the more precise the lifter is in bringing the feet back in line, the faster they can get the down signal. The recovery is more balance and stability dependent than force dependent.

The jerk, unfortunately, has a particular distinction of being a suicide lift, due to the fact that it is more often than not executed with erratic motions. This is in part due to the lifter having to dive under the weight at such a quick change in direction, while splitting the feet apart at the same time, and under some duress of fatigue. That action can cause the weight and the lifter to be out of sync upon receiving the barbell. The lifter never knows what to expect, and has precious little time to make corrections in balance to secure and stand up out of the split. The jerk, unlike the snatch or clean cannot be as controlled a lift, because it only takes .5 seconds to drive and receive the weight. It is therefore essential that every jerk during the incremental increases be executed as fast as possible and received in the exact same position. The lifter should not do a power split jerk during the incremental increases to the top end weight when training the clean & jerk. All the jerks should be executed at the same reception depth from about 70% to the top end weight for that workout session or competition.

What Precision Means

Weightlifting is not a natural phenomenon like running, jumping and throwing. Although the technique of the snatch and clean & jerk is not near as complex as some would argue; what causes the technique to become difficult is the increase in resistance, especially at or near maximal weights. It can and often becomes almost impossible to be exactly precise when attempting maximum weights due to the increased resistance to those motions. The lifter is not only fighting the increased resistance but also the ability of the body to stay precise. It unfortunately becomes easier to allow the weight to control the lifter instead of the lifter controlling the weight.

Another factor concerning technique is the times in motion should be consistent and not change regardless of the weight being lifted. When specific velocities and precise mechanics are not included together it makes it doubly difficult to not only train for the sport of lifting, but to maintain those elements when attempting maximal weights, as well as all previous incremental increases. It is a bit irrelevant how hard or long a lifter trains if all their lifts during training are not executed using consistent velocities along with precise motions.

Section 3: Correlations

Before explaining the various lifts that are essential to the sport, it might be a good idea to understand the basic concepts concerning correlations and ratios with respect to optimal velocity or specific times in motion. Correlations are not based on absolutes, but are generalized inferences. The correlations and ratios I have proposed are close approximations, and are somewhat accurate within a small range of tolerance, but are not infallible. Each individual lifter will have to determine what their ratios are based on their own data with respect to the formulas I have created below.

Correlation 1a: Clean & Jerk to Back Squat ratio

The ratio of a clean & jerk to a back squat, when the time in standing up from a full squat is 1 second would be approximately 86%. Slower times in the back squat can move more weight in a back squat, but the efficiency of motion between a 1second back squat and slower squat is less, and the ration of 86% cannot be attained.

Example: A lifter has a back squat of 200k in 1.6 seconds and has a clean & jerk of 150k. The ratio of clean & jerk to back squat is; 150k / 200k = 75%.

If the lifter in the above example wants to clean & jerk more than 150k then he needs to back squat 180k in 1 second. 180k x .86 = 155k. The decrease from 200k in 1.6 seconds down to 180k in 1 second reduces the stresses on the joints and allows for faster physical recovery from workout to workout.

Correlation 1b: Clean Pull to Back Squat

The clean pull to full extension (without the bending of the arms) should be .67 seconds and this time of .67 seconds should be correlated to a back squat from parallel or just above parallel in 20/30th of a second (.67) with 125% of clean & jerk PR.

Example: 155k clean & jerk PR where the pull to full extension is 20/30th of a second (.67), the back squat from just above parallel should be 125% x 155k = 194k @ .67 seconds.

The clean pulls should not be trained as a dead lift, but trained using the specific time in motion of .67 seconds regardless of the weight on the bar. It does little good to pull more weight slower because that will disrupt the training of the snatch and clean & jerk and squats as well, and place undue stress on the muscular system. Testing to see how much weight can be dead lifted or pulled regardless of the time in motion I would consider to be antagonistic to those bidirectional motions, especially when testing is done too often or as some primary goal.

Correlation 1c: Snatch to clean & jerk

Snatch / C&J = 80%

Example: The lifter with a 150k clean & jerk meet PR, should have a snatch meet PR in the area of: 150k x .8 = 120k.

80% is a normal acceptable approximation of snatch to clean & jerk. The snatch to clean & jerk can be anywhere from 70% to 90%. Anything well outside the acceptable norm of 80% should be looked at carefully and some determination should be made as to whether that can or cannot be corrected. It is rather dubious as to whether correlations can be fixed, because they reflect more than weaknesses, but also contain certain phycological and physiological characteristics of each individual lifter.

Correlation 1d: Snatch pull to clean pull should be 85%

Example: The lifter has a 200k clean pull, thus;
200k x .85 = 170k snatch pull

The reason 85% is used instead of the 80% is because the pulls do not contain the motion of pulling under the weight, so the 1st and 2nd pull are the primary motion in both the snatch and clean pull. Only the width of the grip is a factor. The pulls will be discussed later as to the role they play as an assistance lift.

Equivalent Force Formulas

Equivalent force formulas are based on my hypothesis pertaining to the fast twitch muscle fiber's role in generating momentum from velocity. In weightlifting force is produced at times in motion (t) of less than 1 second and force has to be overcome when those times are slower than 1 second or at the point where the motions of the lifter begins to decelerate. Deceleration is the key element that should not be allowed to occur during any part of any lift or any rep in any set of reps during training.

Formula 2a: To interpolate a back squat slower than 1 second to a 1 second back squat;

Bs - [(t - 1) x 5k] = Bs1

Where (Bs) is the actual amount of weight, (t) is the actual time standing up out of the back squat, and must be slower than 1 second. The difference in the time is multiplied by 5k and this is then subtracted from the original back squat (Bs) to arrive at what the equivalent back squat in 1 second (Bs1) would be.

Example: A back squat is achieved with a weight of 180k in 1.2 seconds.
(1.2 - 1) = 2 (1/10th units) x 5k = 10k, then 180k - 10k = 170k in 1 second.

This means the lifter might have squatted more weight than the 175k PR, but the 180k in 1.2 seconds was not equal to the 175k in 1 second, so the 180k should not be used to determine the correlation between the clean & jerk and back squat, unless the lifter uses 1.2 seconds as a baseline (time index) for the back squat, i.e. the baseline or time in motion should be the determining factor, not just the increase of weight.

Formula 2b: To interpolate a back squat faster than 1 second to a 1 second back squat;

Bs + [(1 - t) x 10k] = Bs1

Where (Bs) is actual amount of back squat, (t) is the actual time of the back squat, and must be faster than 1 second. The difference in the time (1/10th of a second) is multiplied by 10k and this is then added to the original back squat (Bs) to arrive at what the equivalent back squat in 1 second would be (Bs1).

Example: The same lifter who did 180k in 1.2 seconds does 160k in .8 seconds.
1 - .8 = 2 (1/10th of second in units) x 10k = 20k, then 160k + 20k = 180k in 1 second.

In the above example, the 180k is greater than the 175k in 1 second, and the 180k in 1 second would be considered an equivalent time PR, where 160k in .8 seconds is equal to 180k in 1 second. It would not be noted as an actual PR back squat, but would be noted as an equivalent force produced PR back squat in 1 second.

The reason there is 5k per unit when moving slower than 1 second, and 10k per unit when moving faster, is because the fast twitch fibers are 100% in play at faster times in motion than they are at the slower times. The 5k and 10k are used as close approximations for the sake of simplifying the formulas to get close to a somewhat accurate picture. This is not an exact scientific expression because of the many factors among lifters that preclude such exactness to be achieved, however, these formulas are a close approximation of what can be expected.

Formula 2c: To determine force equivalents when reps are achieved and all those reps are executed in 1 second.

Bs + [(r - 1) x 5k] = Bs1

Example 1: The same lifter does 170k x 3 all in 1 second; Bs + 3 reps - 1 rep = 2 units x 5k = 10k + 170k = 180k in 1 second.

Example 2: The same lifter decides to see how much they can back squat regardless of the time in motion, and does 180k x 3 in 2 seconds (average time in motion). Only the standing-up times are used for the average, not the downward times or overall set time. This is important for getting as accurate a result as possible.

Formula 2c gives the rep equivalent as 190k x 1 in 2 seconds. Formula 2b is used to arrive at the equivalent in 1 second which is 140k in 1 second.

This does not mean the lifter can't do more than 140k in 1 second, because that has already been achieved with 175k. It means the 180k x 3 in 2 seconds only produced 140k of force, because the fast twitch were not in play but only for 1 second of the 2 seconds. The other 1 second was slow twitch, therefore the production of force is less.

If the lifter tried to use the 190k rep equivalent, and not time equivalent, as a benchmark for determining how much they could clean & jerk, that would be; 190k x .86 = 163k. While it might be possible for the lifter to achieve the 163k, the overall time in motion could not be maintained at the same time as the 150k, because the 190k was not time equivalent to the 175k.

Example 3: The same lifter does 140k x 5 in .7 seconds for each rep.

Using formula 2c we arrive at 160k x 1 being equivalent to 140k x 5, then using formula 2b we arrive at 190k in 1 second, which is equivalent to the 140k x 5 in .7 seconds (average time per rep).

The above result is a new PR which is time equivalent. 140k x 5 @ .7 seconds ea. is time equivalent to 190k x 1 @ 1 second, and is greater in force than the previous 180k @ 1 second. What needs to occur is the time in motion should stay constant as the weight is increased. The 190k x 1 equivalent should be noted as such next to the actual 140k x 5 @ .7 seconds. The 190k can be used to identify a possible future potential PR clean & jerk or back Squat.

190k x .86 = 163k potential clean & jerk, and 190k potential back squat in 1 second. Obviously the clean & jerk of 163k is more important to achieve than the back squat. This means the squats can be increased by using equivalent times rather than actual amounts of weight, since the back squat is not being contested in competition.

Excess Velocity (Force)

Generally as long as more force is placed into a lift or less time in motion than is needed to make the lift, then excess force is being produced. This means the lifter is simulating moving more weight than is actually loaded on the barbell. Excess force can be measured by using times in motion.

Example: When a lifter is going from 60k to 130k in the snatch, and a unit of force of 1 is equal to 130k in an overall time of 2.5 seconds (from the platform to standing up with the snatch) then excess force can be determined. These are approximate calculations used for simplifying the discussion.

Using the formula F = ma, where (a) is denoted as time in motion, then the equivalent force for a lesser weight could be obtained by doing the following calculations.

F = 130k x 1 = 130
F = 120k x 1.08 = 130
F = 110k x 1.18 = 130
F = 100k x 1.3 = 130
F = 80k x 1.625 = 130
F = 60k x 2.16 = 130

From the above we can determine the time in motion to make each lift equal in force to 130k.

60k is 2.5 / 2.16 = 1.15 sec.
80k is 2.5 / 1.625 = 1.53 sec.
100k is 2.5 / 1.3 = 1.69 sec.
110k is 2.5 / 1.18 = 2.11 sec.
120k is 2.5 / 1.08 = 2.31 sec.
130k is 2.5 / 1 = 2.5 sec.

If 1.7 seconds is close to a maximum achievable overall time, then from 60k to 100k the lifter could not produce excessive force equal to 130k, but should attempt to move at that maximum velocity of 1.7 seconds, in order to produce as much excess force as possible.

This means when moving up in weight from 60k to 130k the lifter will not be able to move fast enough to produce excessive force till they reach 110k. There is only a small difference in weight where equivalent force can be applied. From the empty bar to 60k the lifter need not move any faster than necessary to make the weight. In other words warmup weights should never be achieved at full force or the fastest times in motion possible, but they should be executed at times closer to the times achieved with maximal weights. In this case 2.5 seconds for anything under 60k.

The times in motion might look something like this once the lifter has warmed up;

60k in 1.7 sec.
80k in 1.7 sec.
90k in 1.8 sec.
100k in 1.9 sec.
110k in 2.11 sec.
120k in 2.31 sec.
130k in 2.5 sec.

Above 130k or more might look like this;

140k in 2.7 sec.
150k in 3.0 sec.

As the weight increases the times in motion will begin to get slower exponentially, due to the forces placed on the unidirectional motions, and the lifter is unable to overcome those forces and generate the right velocity during the bidirectional motions. This being the direct cause of most lifts being missed, and not necessarily a problem concerning technique, but a problem concerning the lack of momentum produced during the 1st and 2nd pull from the platform to full extension and/or a slower change in direction pulling under the weight. This can cause what appears to be technical flaws or breakdowns. Somewhere along the trajectory line the accelerated velocity is too slow for the lifter to maintain their particular precision or technical proficiency. Again, while it might look as if the lift was missed due to technical error(s), it was actually missed because there was not enough momentum placed into the weight, i.e., the times in motion are slower.

It is possible to lift more weight in the clean & jerk by moving slower than 2.5 seconds, however, it is not possible to progress to full potential that way. The slower unidirectional motions in the 1st pull and standing up with the weight create a roadblock to progress, and at some point the lifter will begin to stagnate due to those slower times, even if the bidirectional times are in tact. There are greater stresses placed on the bidirectional motions when there is less reliability in overcoming forces. Additional stresses are placed directly into the fast twitch muscle fibers, which have a direct impact on the lifter being able to produce maximal velocities.

Example: The same lifter in the above examples with a 150k clean & jerk decides to start pushing the squats and pulls using slow and grinding motions and eventually is able to clean & jerk 190k, but the overall time is 3.2 seconds. The jerk may or may not be missed, but it will be a more difficult jerk, especially if there is an additional .5 second pause in the bottom of the clean. The more cleans with 190k the lifter does in training using these slower times, then more overloading of the muscular system occurs, because at 3.2 seconds the lifter is actually only producing the forces equivalent to a 155k clean & jerk at 2.5 seconds. Stagnation will and must occur, and 190k will be the lifter's full potential. This is a direct result of doing slow grinding squats and pulls over long periods of time to increase the performance of the clean & jerk. What the lifter should have done was progress the clean & jerk using the 2.5 second overall time and increased the squats and pulls also using specific and consistent times in motion. When the lifter reached 190k in 2.5 seconds the lifter could then continue to progress. Whether stagnation can be corrected by starting over and training correctly by using constant times in motion instead of increases regardless of those times in motion is questionable. Once a lifter has accepted certain methodologies of training, it becomes near impossible to pry them away from the comfort of their own training methods, even if those methods are not yielding any progress.

Note: Stagnation is not a good or bad term. It means that some lifters have reached their full potential and need simply maintain what they have achieved for as long as possible. Becoming stagnant before full potential is reached is not good. Stagnation does not mean the lifter does not make a few kilos of progress here and there, it means that generally their progress has reached a tipping point where they no longer will be on a consistent and continuous path of progressing their performance, and there might well be wild and erratic swings in performance from meet to meet and in training.

By applying excess force to each weight more work is applied to the training load without adding more weight. The additional simulated mass helps develop the lifter's muscular system by way of the fast and slow twitch fibers, but there is no overloading or stress placed on the muscles, unless the times are slower than 2.5 seconds, then gradually from 2.5 seconds the overloading increases.

The squats should look something like the list below when warming up to 175k in 1 second while applying excessive force (accelerated velocity) from 135k and up.

75k in .5 seconds
95k in .5 seconds
115k in .5 seconds
135k in .6 seconds
155k in .8 seconds
175 in 1 second

As the weight increases past 1 second the times start to drop off exponentially till the lifter is unable to move at all through the sticking point. If the lifter trains the fast and slow twitch using 1 second times, and no absolute weight is ever handled, then it becomes even more difficult to move more weight slower, because the muscles have not been trained or developed for that purpose. The lifter might be unable to squat slower than 1.3 seconds without decelerating considerably at the sticking point. This is exactly what needs to happen. It is a sure sign the lifter has been developing and training the muscles to move at specific velocities. The specific velocities become more ingrained and the sticking point is dissolved away almost completely. The squats and pulls are for all intent and purpose used by the weightlifter for one goal, and that goal is to increase the ability of the lifter to handle more weight in the snatch and clean & jerk, and still maintain the same times in motion.

If this lifter increases their full upright back squat to 220k in 1 second, then 190k can be achieved in 2.5 seconds or faster and the lifter can continue to progress both the clean & jerk and the back squat using those specific velocities for each lift. In this case their back squat would look something like the following;

150k in .5 sec.
170k in .5 sec.
180k in .6 sec.
200k in .8 sec.
210k in .9 sec.
220k in 1 sec.

As mentioned earlier, the times in motion are still around 10k per 1/10th of a second, and possibly even from about 1.3 seconds or faster, regardless of the level the lifter has attained. Variations to the 1/10th per second would be on an individual basis and more than likely be dependent on the fast to slow twitch muscle fiber ratio, which determine the quicker reaction times for changes in direction and accelerated velocities.

The correlations between lifts must be resolved from specific times in motion being at a fairly constant and consistent value, for those correlations to hold up to a high standard of accuracy. If the times in motion overly vary among the unidirectional and bidirectional motions, then those correlations will also vary and it will become more difficult to pin down a meaningful ratio. The same would be true for erratic lifting from one rep to the next. Progress has to come from technical precision and some consistency in the times in motion of all the primary lifts.

Section 4: Time (t) Index

In individual sports and some team sports the coach is always poised with stopwatch in hand to record certain aspects of the athlete's performance. In track and swimming the coach times the athlete in order to determine the quality of the training and in order to get the athlete in shape. It would be near impossible for a coach or athlete to know where they were with respect to training without timing their laps. The stop watch is more widely used in sports than any other instrument. The reason for measuring performance using time or a stopwatch, is because the value of (t) time is used in all formulas where force, power, speed (mph), torque and accelerated velocity are calculated. While measuring a performance using time may not give the most exact scientific measurement, it does give a general value that makes taking measurements less complex and more readily available and understood. It's more convenient for Usain Bolt to know how fast he ran a particular distance in training than to know what his top speed was or how much force during any particular stride he was producing.

The stopwatch is rarely used in weightlifting. Expensive computer applications and equipment are more commonly used, mainly because time in motion during a snatch, clean & jerk, squat and pull is not seen the same as timing laps on a track or in a pool. If, however, a lifter does not know how fast they can move during a primary lift they will be completely in the dark as to their overall training, because of equivalent force from inequivalent times.

Each individual athlete has a built in ability to produce a certain amount of accelerated velocity. The ability to move at a certain accelerated velocity is called reaction time. Other factors such as fast and slow twitch distribution also effect reaction time. Suffice it to say, once full development has been reached the athlete may not be able to increase their reaction time, especially when all their skills are honed in to perfection.

In order for the weightlifter to continue to progress they must be able to achieve the snatch or clean at their established **Time Index (TI)** regardless of the weight on the bar. From the platform to full extension a TI of .67 seconds is the most common time among the vast majority of top lifters when handling up to 100% of PR. Time indexes can vary from .6 seconds to .8 seconds and each individual lifter must discover their own TI by measuring their top end lifts each training session.

The time index should be applied to the squats and pulls in order to keep all the primary lifts in equilibrium and keep the squats and pulls as true assistance lifts instead of training those lifts like a powerlifter would. The sports of powerlifting and weightlifting are not compatible. Training the squats and pulls as in powerlifting will only create mediocrity between the squats, pulls and competition lifts.

If a lifter has a TI of .67 seconds for their clean (I would use the clean TI rather than the snatch), then that .67 seconds should be the limiting factor for doing squats from parallel and pulls to full extension. Progressing the squat and pull is more efficient when progressing those lifts through the TI instead of by how much weight can be handled regardless of time. This particular time in motion of .67 seconds needs to be ingrained so perfectly that the lifter will not be able to move at a slower time during the snatch or clean & jerk regardless of the weight on the bar or if they do move slower they will readily feel it and will know not to increase the weight further. Missing a lift is usually always a result of the lifter not applying the correct velocity, and not a flaw in their technique, although technique should include the lifter's particular time in motion.

Example 1: A lifter has a clean & jerk PR of 150k and his TI is .67 seconds and overall time in motion (from the platform to standing up with the clean) of 2.2 seconds. The only way this lifter can achieve the 2.2 overall time is to be able to pull 150k or a bit more in .67 seconds, and front squat from at least parallel 150k in .67 seconds.

The main thing to remember when doing a snatch or clean & jerk is that regardless of the weight on the bar the velocity of the lifter will always be finite based on their ability to accelerate from 0 to their particular TI. The slower that motion deviates from their normal TI the greater chance of missing the lift. The TI is more important with weights in excess of 80% of PR. Less than 80% the lifter can move slower and still make the weight as long as the velocity produces the momentum needed to make the weight.

Example 2: The same lifter as above is training at 85% of PR for three singles, which would be around 128k. Since they are handling more than 80% of PR they will need to move at .67 seconds from the platform to full extension to make the lift, if they move to full extension at .8 seconds instead then two things will happen: 1) The weight will feel heavier, because slower times decreases force, and 2) The weight could be flat out missed, because their TI was not achieved. These things become more pronounced as the weight reaches 100% of PR.

Most lifters are taught that they have to squat and pull a lot of weight in order to get strong. The problem with this concept is the word "strong" is not defined which makes the phrase "a lot of weight" an irrational thought. While there is no question that the lifter will be better off squatting and pulling more than 100% of their PR clean, that more than 100% must also contain the lifters TI for it to be equivalent. The idea that more is better is a false assumption, when more is slower than the TI. Slower grinding motions become antagonistic to that TI. The lifter winds up chasing their tail because trying to squat more weight regardless of how slow it is does not work the fast twitch correctly and the snatch and clean & jerk motions are interfered with and can and often do decline or become stagnant or very slow to progress. This is the problem with so called strength cycles or squat routines based solely on moving more weight regardless of time in motion. Without doubt the lifter can easily increase their squat when their time in motion is decreased, but the impact this has on the snatch and clean & jerk is the opposite and while they are getting "stronger" by lifting more weight slower, their time index is getting slower.

In effect, the primary lifts should be trained using the lifter's particular TI. In essence, the squats and pulls are the only parts of the snatch and clean & jerk that need to be executed, always being mindful to adhere to that TI. The snatch and clean & jerk should always be executed off the platform, not from a deficit, boxes or from the hang. These types of partial motions create different neurological pathways which interfere with the overall motion of the full movement, as well as the TI.

It's not my intention to take away some of the lifters playthings, but only to bring some awareness of the reality contained in the sport. Most, if not all, auxiliary exercises were created from warmup exercises with the empty bar. These exercises become fads where top lifters are seen trying to execute these exercises with maximal weight. The muscle snatch is a good example. The muscle snatch is actually a stiff legged snatch, and as the weight increases the weight is caught lower and lower until it becomes a snatch grip press out of huge proportions and at that point does not resemble a snatch by any stretch of the imagination.

Instead of wasting time trying to set PRs off boxes, from the hang or with the myriad of auxiliary exercises I would advise using that time trying to hone in specific skills doing the full movements and the squats and pulls using their particular TI.

Section 5: F = ma

Sir Isaac Newton's 2nd law of motion (F = ma) is a reflexion of how a weightlifter should go about training their squats and pulls. Where force (F) is the result of a change in acceleration (a), generated against a mass (m) or the weight of the barbell. Since generally all snatches and cleans from the platform to receiving the weight are achieved in about 1 second, then acceleration (a) is constant, and force (F) will always equal mass (m) or the weight on the barbell. Since the snatch and clean must be achieved in about 1 second, regardless of the increase in that weight, then the accelerated mass will always equal the force and equilibrium is reached. When a lift is missed due to the lifter being unable to overcome the forces placed on their body, and therefore the inability to achieve the correct velocity, then the change in velocity is slower, which then decreases the force production (F), and the lifter and the weight are out of equilibrium.

It is not so much a question of being strong enough to achieve a particular amount of weight, as it is being conditioned enough to maintain the .67 second time in motion from the platform to full extension in the snatch and clean & jerk. A good example is a shot putter. When the weight of the shot put was 8 pounds, 12 pounds and 16 pounds, from junior high to college, the difference was 4 pounds between each of the implements used at the various scholastic levels. Most shot putters have about a 10 foot difference between those implements. If a high school shot putter could throw the 12 pounder 60 feet, they could throw the 8 pound shot 70 feet and the 16 pound shot 50 feet. The difference in distance was due to the fact that they could only overcome equivalent forces for each implement, based on their ability to accelerate their body. If they could generate the same speed as they did when throwing the 8 pound shot 70 feet, when throwing the 16 pound shot put, they could theoretically throw the 16 pounder 70 feet also. It is the ability to generate and unleash torque that produces a particular distance. As the shot putter moves from junior high to college, they have to overcome greater forces in order to maintain the same velocity in the ring to achieve the same distance they achieved in high school, or from junior high to high school.

Increasing one's ability to overcome greater forces without increasing or maintaining specific accelerated velocities is of little use to the individual athlete, with the exception of the powerlifter. Powerlifting skills are dependent on slower changes in acceleration in order to decrease the additional forces placed on the body of the powerlifter as the weight increases. The more the weight is increased, then less force is placed on the muscular system through a decrease in acceleration or time in motion. This is a concern of the slow twitch muscle fibers, because the fast twitch are rarely used in powerlifting, or they are used up very early on. All other individual sports, where a bidirectional motion is used, require equilibrium between force and changes in acceleration, and both muscle fibers must be trained to move faster than what the athlete is ultimately able to control effectively.

As explained earlier, certain parts of the lifts contain both bidirectional and unidirectional motions. The 1st pull in the snatch and clean is unidirectional, but is preceded by a bidirectional motion or gathering of forces just before lift-off. The 2nd and 3rd pull in the snatch and clean are bidirectional motions where momentum is produced in order to receive the weight at some point in the trajectory, i.e., high snatch or clean or full squat snatch or clean. The recovery from a full squat is a unidirectional motion, with exceptions. A timed rebound and a forced rebound are bidirectional motions where greater momentum is achieved over a static recovery. The gathering of forces occurs right before the timed rebound in the snatch or clean to ready the lifter for the rebound. The jerk drive is a bidirectional motion, because momentum must be produced from the dip or change in direction. Recovery of the jerk is unidirectional, with little or no time restrictions placed on that recovery, other than those imposed on the lifter to control the weight before getting the down signal.

The pulls contain the same pulling motions as the snatch and clean & jerk. There can be no deviation between the pulls and competition lifts, with regard to the 1st and 2nd pull. Since the lifter is never executing the 3rd pull when doing pulls, the arms should always be kept straight through full extension. Snatch high pulls are of little value other than as a warmup exercise using the empty bar or less than 50%. The lifter should never allow the arms to bend when doing pulls where there is no effort to pull under the weight. It can be debated whether a simulated effort to pull under the weight is useful, practical, feasible or even possible. I think it's highly unlikely. The high elbow high pull is a good warmup exercise and helps keep the shoulder girdle stretched out, but should not be used to pull near maximal weights, because that motion is not the same as the one used during the 3rd pull.

Specific Times in Motion for Training Purposes

Snatch: From the platform to standing up with the weight should take about 2 to 2.5 seconds with a timed rebound and without a pause or balance check in the bottom position. 2.5 seconds was researched as the minimum time limit for most of the top lifters in the world. See last section in book for sample times in motion of a few of the top lifters in the world.

Clean: From the platform to standing up with the weight should take about 2 to 2.5 seconds with a timed rebound.

Jerk: From the lowest trajectory point in the dip to receiving the weight to a fully locked out position, should take about .5 seconds.

Snatch Pull: From the platform to full extension should be close to .67 seconds. Without a 3rd pull there is no change in direction and some floating will occur at full extension. The time should be measured from the platform to the power position.

Clean Pull: From the platform to full extension should take .67 second, but could be a bit faster due to the narrower grip and higher hip starting position. Both the snatch and clean should be carefully timed over enough workouts to determine each lifters TI (Time Index).

Front Squat: Controlled downward motion, and 1 second or faster when standing up. When doing reps the recovery times should remain as consistent as possible, from the first rep to the last. The overall time of both the downward and upward motion can be 2 to 2.5 seconds.

Back Squat (full): Controlled downward motion, and 1 second or faster in the upward motion. When doing reps the stand-up times should remain constant regardless of the weight on the bar or the number of reps or sets.

Back Squat (just above parallel): Controlled downward motion, and .67 seconds or faster in the upward motion. When doing reps the stand-up times should all be the same regardless of the weight on the bar or the number of reps or sets.

Note: The phrase "regardless of the weight on the bar" simply means the lifter should feel free to load as much weight on the bar as possible as long as those times in motion associated with any particular lift are maintained. Once the lifter feels those times slowing down, no further increase on the bar should be made and the exercise is over, aside from doing down sets if applicable.

Those motions which require an extension of the body, and momentum and/or inertia to be generated are bidirectional motions. Those motions which do not generate momentum and/or inertia are unidirectional motions.

Most all team sports are composed of bidirectional motions, i.e., running, throwing and/or jumping. Pushing an opponent, as in football, is bidirectional, swinging a baseball bat is bidirectional, due to the motion of the baseball going up and down, achieving both momentum and inertia. The batter generates momentum through the swing of the bat, called "bat speed". That momentum is transferred into the ball on contact. A discus thrower produces momentum by unleashing torque, between the upper and lower body, and that momentum is transferred into the discus which causes the discus to achieve a particular flight or trajectory. In weightlifting the lifter must catch their own implement so the upward and downward motion is confined to the trajectory of the lifter. The flight of the barbell on it's own would be from full extension to the highest trajectory point, if the grip were released at full extension the barbell would immediately cease traveling upward.

Powerlifting is mostly unidirectional, where there is no timed rebound in that action, or an attempt to increase momentum or generate inertia. While a decrease in momentum is beneficial in powerlifting, it can be anti-productive to other athletes who rely on greater changes in acceleration, during a change in direction.

Acceleration is a change in velocity over distance, and in weightlifting, that acceleration is reached at a very quick rate of change, through what is called "thrust" and velocities are almost instantly reached as the lifter begins the pull off the platform, and also during the recovery in the front squat and clean, as well as the drive in the jerk. The pull does not become a bidirectional motion until momentum is generated from the 2nd pull, at which point it changes from unidirectional to bidirectional. Maximum momentum occurs when the lifter's hips are pushed forward and the lifter reaches full extension.

Reaction time is a concern of timing and balance while the changes in acceleration are going on during the lift. If any particular phase of the pull needs to be executed at the quickest change of direction it should be the 3rd pull, because the lifter needs to pull under the weight as quickly as is possible (.33 seconds or faster) before the inertia runs out or the weight begins to move downward before the lifter is in position for the catch.

The squats and pulls are, by nature themselves, not bound by the same principles as the bidirectional motions. Greater weights can be achieved in the squats and pulls by moving as slow as the lifter can move and still make the weight. In powerlifting the force is decreased as the mass increases, and the velocity decreases. This is ideal for powerlifting, where only the amount of weight lifted matters, but in weightlifting, there are bidirectional motions that have to be considered, which the powerlifter does not have to deal with. This again ties into the concept of the squats and pulls being functional to the competition lifts and not just as a means of handling bigger weights without regard for the times in motion or the technical proficiency or precision of those squats and pulls.

Training the squats and pulls and snatch and clean & jerk using specific times in motion instead of purely how much weight can be moved can be a difficult concept to get across to lifters who believe that the only thing that matters is how much weight is lifted regardless of technical precision or specific times in motion.

A decent level of performance can be reached training the squats and pulls using maximum efforts regardless of precision or the use of specific times in motion. The only problem is the lifter might well reach a decent level of performance, but will not and cannot ever reach their full potential, and they will become stagnant earlier than if they trained using precision and specific times in motion.

When the weightlifter tries to move as fast as they possibly can in the snatch and clean, from the empty bar to maximum amount of weight, the changes in velocity can be faster from the empty bar and become slower as the weight increases, however, the overall times in motion should remain fairly constant from 70% to the final weight lifted. The overall time of 2.5 seconds from the platform to standing up with the weight includes the 1st pull, 2nd pull, 3rd pull, securing the weight and standing up with the weight. The pull from the platform to full extension should be .67 seconds with maximal weights. The 1st pull is .5 seconds, the 2nd pull .17 seconds and the 3rd pull .33 seconds. I call these the golden ratios of weightlifting. 1st pull to second pull is approx. 3 to 1, 2nd pull to 3rd pull is 1 to 2 (.17 to .33) and 1st and 2nd pull (from platform to full extension) to 3rd pull is 2 to 1 (.67 to .33). Again, it is up to the lifter to measure their times in motion in order to establish their own times in motion which can be applied to the squats and pulls.

Thrust is achieved in the recovery by using a timed rebound out of the bottom from the reaction of the catch into the bottom. The rebound is timing intense and must be practiced when doing front squats out of the rack and during the clean and the snatch from the platform. The timed rebound is action/reaction based because once the gathering of forces phase is commenced the action of the rebound cannot be stopped.

If the lifter uses slow and grinding actions (deceleration) when doing squats and pulls (dead lifts), they will lift slow in the 1st pull and standing up with the weight will also be slower and grinding. It may not effect the velocity of the 2nd and 3rd pull, but it will keep the lifter from reaching their full potential, because it's the overall time in motion of at least 2.5 seconds that needs to be maintained at maximal weights in order to leave room to progress to higher levels.

It does little good to be just as strong as another lifter, but not be faster, because the faster lifter will always have an advantage over the slower lifter. The definition of strength, as far as the sport of weightlifting is concerned, has to include the specific velocity or the overall times in motion of the lift. Whether weightlifting is a speed sport or strength sport has always been debated. I believe the answer is speed, because it is speed or velocity that defines what the word "strength" means to the weightlifter.

Measuring Time in Motion

In order to time a lifter's motions in various phases of a lift, or the overall lift, all that is needed is a 30 fps small hand held camera, or phone camera. Once the video has been transferred to a computer, then each frame is 1/30th of a second or each click on the forward arrow key. When the bar begins to move upward start clicking one frame at a time and begin counting. When the bar reaches its highest trajectory stop clicking and counting. 30 frames (clicks) is

1 second and 36 frames (clicks) is 1.2 seconds. Just divide the number of frames counted by 30 to arrive at the time it takes to recover the squat or execute the pull through the different phases, to arrive at the appropriate times in motion.

Section 6: The Primary Lifts

The lifts a weightlifter orders in training all have a very specific purpose and are designed to create an overall system (program) which can be used to establish goals, monitor progress and train and peak for competition. All the lifts that are chosen should be categorized as to their importance, validity or necessity.

Most athletes have to generate force through their own body, such as gymnasts, divers, competitive swimmers and track and field athletes, to name a few. In the case of track and field, the athletes who throw implements not only have to generate force, but overcome those forces created by the additional weight of the implement they are throwing. The pole vaulter also has to overcome the forces created by the pole they carry, which propels them over the crossbar. Not much different from those forces that have to be overcome when a rocket is attempting to reach escape velocity by overcoming the gravitational pull of the Earth. The thrust of the rockets have to overcome both the Earth's gravity and the weight of the rocket.

Producing force is confined to the bidirectional motions contained in the 2nd and 3rd pull and the timed rebound motion, also the drive in the jerk, and receiving the jerk. Bidirectional velocities are inherent to each individual lifter, and those specific times in motion must be fixed at the fastest controllable value possible. Bidirectional velocities cannot be increased once the lifter has fully developed. The unidirectional motions surrounding those bidirectional motions, i.e., the 1st pull, recovery after the timed rebound, the dip in the jerk and the jerk recovery, should always remain in agreement with the bidirectional velocities.

The weightlifter will reach full development, pertaining to maximum available bidirectional velocities, before reaching their full potential pertaining to the maximum amount of weight they will lift. It takes longer to increase the size and strength (overcoming forces) and velocity of the muscular system than it does to develop maximum reaction time.

No matter how many repetitions of the bidirectional motion are executed, there will not be any direct increase in gains from those repetitions if all those repetitions are not achieved using a constant and consistent velocity. Gains in performance also come from increasing the unidirectional velocities contained in the squats and pulls, which can be used to maintain those bidirectional velocities as the weight increases. Conditioning (getting in shape) and keeping the snatch and clean & jerk honed in are the indirect results of volume vs velocity. Without an increase in the squats and pulls, using a consistent measure of velocity, there will be no increase in the snatch and clean & jerk, once the lifter has reached full development with respect to the bidirectional velocities, i.e., the lifter's maximum reaction time.

Only a beginner will achieve gains in performance by only executing the snatch and clean & jerk. This is because the squats and pulls that are contained in those snatches and clean & jerks are sufficient to increase performance up to the point where the amount of velocity needed for the unidirectional motions begin to exceed the lifter's capabilities. At that point the lifter is no longer bound by the snatch and clean & jerk as the mechanism that will increase performance, but there is a shift towards the unidirectional motions contained in the squats and pulls as the mechanism that will increase performance. This shift will occur regardless of how much more weight can be handled in the squats and pulls relative to the snatch or clean & jerk. This is seen in lifters who switch from powerlifting to weightlifting. No matter how much weight they could move as a powerlifter there is a learning curve that the powerlifter must go through, the same as any beginner, with respect to the snatch and clean & jerk. How much weight the powerlifter was before able to squat or pull (dead lift) becomes somewhat irrelevant and can only be correlated to what they are capable of snatching and clean & jerking at the time.

The notion that all a lifter has to do is increase the squats and pulls by weight only in order to automatically increase the snatch and clean & jerk is false. The squats and pulls are assistance lifts and should not be pushed past certain limitations based on the clean & jerk. For the back squat that limitation should be around 125% of clean & jerk and for the front squat 110%. As the clean & jerk increases then the limitations based on those percentages will increase and the snatch will increase as the clean & jerk increases. It is within these limitations that the 1 second time in motion can be maintained along with the .67 seconds for the pulls and jerk drive.

The greatest detriment to any athlete's future progress is if they begin training too long, too hard and training at 100%

of effort too often, before they learn the skills necessary to actually begin that type of training. It does an athlete little good to halfway learn a new skill or event and then begin training that event at 100% effort, in hopes they will eventually become more technically proficient. Once the athlete begins to train at 100% effort, they will lock in their technical skills at those 100% efforts, and it will be increasingly difficult for them to become more proficient. This should be a concern to all athletes, not just the weightlifter. It is more difficult and takes longer to train an athlete toward technical proficiency when training is 100% of effort, than it is to learn how to be technically proficient in the beginning at much less than 100% efforts, and then begin training after those skills have been effectively ingrained to be as efficient as possible.

There are six primary lifts that must take precedent over all other lifts or exercises. There should be no exceptions. There are slight variations within these six lifts, which will also be discussed. The six primary lifts are as follows;

1) Snatch
2) Clean & Jerk
3) Front Squat
4) Back Squat
5) Snatch
6) Clean Pulls

The beginner has to learn how to do the above six lifts with technical skill, precision and speed (specific times in motion). The squats and pulls should be trained after the clean & jerk as a progression of the incremental increase in order to link the squats and pulls to the snatch and clean & jerk.

In order for the squats and pulls to be executed with technical proficiency, the lifter must become proficient in the snatch and clean & jerk. This is because the technique used in the competition lifts is that same technique they will be using in the squats and pulls. The squats must be executed using the same recovery technique and upright position used in the snatch and clean, and the pulls must be executed the exact same way the lifter does their 1st and 2nd pull in the snatch and clean, regardless of the amount of weight on the bar or the variation of those pulls.

If a beginner learns how to snatch and clean & jerk with perfection, but does the squats and pulls differently from their established technique in the competition lifts, or executes those lifts using slow and/or grinding actions, then they will create a situation where some degradation will occur in some phases within the competition lifts. Acceleration and timing problems can creep into the competition lifts, but worst of all the lifter will not be able to reach their full potential.

Technique can be more easily managed by establishing minimum requirements that should be achieved, rather than trying to explain all the technical nuances of a lift, that often times does little more than confuse the lifter.

1) The fully extended position should be reached in .67 seconds and the pull under the weight in .33 seconds or less.

2) Jumping too far back or forward than acceptable to the individuals preference.

3) The snatch should be received in the full squat position and at parallel in the clean, at which point both lifts should be executed with a timed rebound.
4) The overall time in motion in the snatch and clean should be 2.5 seconds or faster.

5) Standing up from a snatch or clean should be achieved using a timed rebound.

6) Taking steps forward or backward should be avoided or even considered as a missed lift for training purposes.

The lifter will know immediately if they pulled correctly, because in order to meet those requirements stated above, they are almost forced to pull correctly or as efficiently as is possible for their ability and style of lifting.

It's the responsibility of the lifter to learn how to do their event, with the help of a coach or adviser, and it's the responsibility of the coach to understand the relationship between all the primary lifts, and train the lifter accordingly. The coach must show the lifter the correct positions to be in during a lift, but the lifter must take full responsibility as to how they go about perfecting those positions. The more a coach gets involved with the lifter's style or form the less the lifter can figure things out on their own, as far as what might work best for them.

If the squats and pulls are not executed correctly it will not matter how technically proficient the lifter is in the competition lifts, because the lifter can reach a point of stagnation very quickly, if the squats and pulls are not executed correctly. It's up to the coach or trainer to make sure the lifter is executing all the primary lifts with exacting precision and consistent times in motion. The competition lifts can only become more proficient if the squats and pulls are executed proficiently, but it cannot be the other way around. A lifter can become exceptionally proficient in the competition lifts, but if the squats and pulls are not executed with equal proficiency, all will be for naught, as far as a lifter developing their full potential. Perfect technique does not and cannot guarantee the lifter will progress to full potential. Perfect technique only gives the lifter a small advantage toward that end but they are still obligated to train correctly or it will matter little how pretty their lifting looks.

As soon as a lifter becomes skilled at all six primary lifts, then training can be commenced. Gradual, consistent and continuous progress should be made in all of the primary lifts in a close unison of progression. Training should never become a mad rush to set gym PRs, but for the sole purpose of getting in shape and peaking for the major competitions and particular local meets.

The primary lifts are the key to becoming a successful weightlifter. There are variations to the primary lifts, but those variations are somewhat minor in scope, but necessary. It is important to understand that becoming proficient at something takes many repetitions doing the same thing over and over again. No one can say for sure if partial lifts or certain auxiliary exercises are beneficial or not, without a considerable amount of research. I do know that once the lifter has squeezed out as much gains as they can from doing mostly just snatches and clean & jerks those lifts will stagnate, if from that point on the squats and pulls are not increased by weight and specific velocities. The amount of energy stores a lifter has available is what determines how long and intense that training will be.

One cannot adjust to an automatic reduction in intensity, i.e., training while the lifter is in a state of being overtrained or close to it, will not increase performance. More is never better if that more causes the training to be less efficient. It is not possible for beginners or any lifter who has not reached full potential to train like a lifter who has reached that full potential. If the beginner or the lifter that has not yet reached their full potential begins to train like one who has, they will be on the road toward stagnation, before their full potential is reached. This means that at each level of proficiency there has to be clear and concise limitations placed on the amount of weight lifted, and the volume. Training has to take into account both precision and velocity for all the primary lifts. The squats and pulls should never be thought of as slow lifts for any reason whatsoever.

A beginner at age 12 should be limited to weights they can achieve with exacting repeated precision in all the primary lifts and auxiliary exercises. Velocity should become ingrained and consistent within the scope of those limitations. If the limitation is set at 2.2 seconds in the overall time in motion of the snatch and clean, then the beginner should not increase the weight unless that increase is tied to the same 2.2 seconds. The same for the 1 second squats and .67 second pulls to full extension. Velocity is more important for the beginner than the amount of weight. As the lifter advances both the amount of weight and the velocity become important, but the amount of weight alone should never take precedence regardless of what level the lifter has achieved.

The primary lifts should be the only lifts a beginner executes in training until they have ingrained their style and their technical precision can be repeated consistently in all the primary lifts. From there certain auxiliary exercises can be included, but only if those auxiliary exercises are beneficial for the additional foundational support of the lifter. Most exercises or lifts outside the primary lifts cannot be quantified as to their reliability or redundancy of the system; it can, in most cases, only be assumed.

Section 7: The Front and Back Squat

The squats are oftentimes thought of as strength lifts, but in order to overcome forces the accelerated velocity has to also be taken into account, therefore strength needs to be quantified as being both an increase in weight while maintaining the same time in motion from one increase to another. Increases in weight coupled with slower times in motion does not make a lifter stronger it makes them slower.

The Front Squat

The front squat's primary purpose is to make the recovery from the clean as effortless as possible in order to benefit the jerk. Both the snatch and clean & jerk contain a squat in the form of a recovery, sometimes after a timed rebound.

In order for the lifter to get the most benefit from the front squat, they should execute the front squat with their own particular style and posture they use when recovering a clean. This is extremely important. If there is any advantage in motion when doing the front squat over the way the lifter recovers the clean, that can effect the progress of the clean & jerk. It is always more beneficial to execute the front squat using slightly less of a beneficial motion, such as attempting to stay as upright as possible when standing up.

As hard as a lifter tries to mimic the recovery from a clean doing front squats out of the rack, it is just not the same. Cleaning a weight into a full front squat position is a little different from taking the weight out of a rack and then squatting down and up with it. It is easier to do more weight out of a rack than it is to recover the weight after a clean. There must be some understanding of the relationship between the front squat out of the rack and the clean into a rebound position in order to quickly stand up and ready the jerk. The front squat should be executed with little or no deceleration over the amount of weight on the bar.

Example: A lifter with a 200k front squat in 1 second can clean & jerk 182k. This lifter can try and do more weight in the front squat as long as they maintain the 1 second recovery time. In most cases, since the front squat out of the rack is easier to perform than the front squat after the clean, the front squat in 1 second should be about 110% greater than the clean & jerk. In this instance 182k x 110% = 200k in 1 second.

While executing a front squat, the foot placement should be the same as the lifter will have during the recovery from the clean, not during the pull. The hand spacing should also be the same as that used during the recovery from the clean, not when doing the jerk. Variations on foot placement should be executed occasionally to work those muscles when the feet are spread apart very wide when catching a snatch or clean.

The lifter should maintain an erect and rigid posture throughout the lift, keeping the elbows stationary in relation to the upper torso, the chest out and upward, and the back arched. The elbows should remain in the exact same position from start to finish during the execution of the lift. The lifter should keep a forward looking position with the head and eyes. The lifter should make a smooth and controlled entry into the parallel position, and then execute a timed rebound out of the bottom position; achieving the transitional rebound with smooth and continuous acceleration. Again all downward motions in the front squat should be controlled. There are variations to the depths that can be used when executing the front and back squat, but the timed rebound should be used regardless of the depth of the squat, in other words the change in direction should be as quick as possible regardless of the depth. Pausing in the bottom will not and cannot do anything for the lifter except make standing up slower than when no pause is used. Pausing motions would be more correctly used during warmups with 60% or less.

The more upright the lifter is during the downward and upward motions the better. Leaning forward can be corrected, but can be corrected best using light weights in order to force the flexibility. The back can still be arched and the chest held up in a stable position during the front squat, even if the lifter leans forward. It is very important that the lifter's upper toro becomes vertical in the full squat position, right before the timed rebound is initiated.

Note: When lifters change certain aspects of the squats in order to handle more weight, without regard to the correct positions or velocities, they are in essence cheating themselves out of the benefits they could derive from those squats. This type of cheating includes slower recovery times as well as changing the angle of the back and doing a crash dive into the bottom in order to gain an advantage in the rebound. The lifter should hold themselves to a very high standard of performance at all times, and not continually do things wrong and then say what they should have done right. Do it right all the time.

Controlled downward velocities, during the front squat, is beneficial for the dip in the jerk, and catching the weight in the snatch and clean and in the jerk. The drive velocity for the jerk should be .67 seconds from a parallel front squat with 100% PR clean & jerk weight. Note the drive velocity (time in motion) is the same as the pull to full extension. This means the lifter should be able to front squat from parallel 100% of clean & jerk weight in .67 seconds, in order to assure the jerk drive velocity will be in equilibrium.

Note: I use time in motion instead of actual velocity or meters per second (m/sec), because the time in motion is much easier to measure than trying to figure out the actual velocity at any given point. The time in motion covers the whole distance the barbell is moving and velocity or meters per second covers just the absolute velocity at any given point. It is also easier to ascertain the time in motion without the need for force plates or other expensive equipment. Regardless of what equations are used to figure force or power the time (t) in motion over a particular distance must be known.

The lifter should never crash dive into the full squat position, faster than the recovery, nor try and hard bounce out of the bottom position. The crash dive does not work the muscles properly for the dip and drive of the jerk or for receiving the snatch and clean, and for overcoming the sticking point.

Another reason it is not advisable to crash dive into the bottom during a front or back squat, is the forces are increased on the lifter when they reach the full squat position. They have to use a hard rebound out of the bottom to make up for the crash dive forces. In the clean the lifter is only going into the bottom position from a lower level than they do in the downward motion of a front squat. From about parallel to full should be a more controlled and smooth entry. The shock of catching the weight is absorbed by the legs at parallel through the full squat position. The shock cannot be absorbed by crash diving into the bottom, but will generate more stress on the muscular system than is necessary or warranted.

The hard bounce out of the front squat will only get a lifter to a bit above parallel, but if these hard bounces are developed through slower velocities, the lifter will decelerate somewhere at the sticking point. They might also have a tendency to lean forward enough to get through the sticking point. The sticking point cannot be overcome by slower times in the recovery than 1 second. The sticking point has to be overcome by moving faster, without a crash drive or hard bounce, and by keeping the upper torso as vertical as possible and the chest held very upright and stable. Without using a controlled entry into the bottom position of the squat those muscles needed for a timed rebound will not be trained properly.

It is important to conserve as much energy as possible, throughout a lift, especially the clean and jerk. A grinding, or longer than necessary clean recovery, will more often than not translate into a missed jerk. Rule of thumb: a quicker clean will usually equal an easier jerk, at the very least give the lifter a better chance at completing a jerk more efficiently. By quicker clean I am referring to the overall time in motion of 2.5 seconds or faster (from the platform to standing up with the weight).

The back should remain arched or rigid, and the upper torso vertical, to effect a disadvantage directed mainly through the legs and less of an advantage through the back. Without the rigidity and arch in the back, the lifter must change that advantage to other muscles, which can afford an added advantage in order to quickly rebound out of the bottom position and get through the sticking point.

Some slight forward lean is unavoidable, but it should be achieved with an erect and rigid posture. The lifter should only use weights which allow them to achieve these mechanics in order to be able to develop the speed to eventually by-pass the sticking point. The sticking point is from parallel to about quarter squat position. This is the area where the speed can slow down during the recovery, and the slower the recovery the longer the lifter is in the sticking point. If the motion is halted, within the sticking point, the lifter will most likely not be able to stand up with the weight.

The best way to address the sticking point, is to handle weights in training which do not cause the lifter's form or posture to ever be slowed or break down. If the lifter stays within the boundaries of the 1 second recovery time and maintains precision those levels of resistance should not be reached which will cause the lifter to break form or use slower times in the recovery. The pulls will also help strengthen the sticking point to some degree, especially the snatch pulls, where a lower starting position is used.

The amount of weight handled in the front squat should never become so great as to cause the lifter any anxiety over missing the lift. If they need spotters while attempting a front squat, then they are handling too much weight. There is no benefit to a lifter to increase a weight to the point where it might be missed, due to the application of slower speeds. Once a lifter begins handling weights in training that cause form or posture breakdowns, erratic lifting to occur, lifts to be missed and subsequent reps to be slower than the first rep, the lifter is training at too high a level of intensity for those working weights to be effective.

There is no reason any squat should ever be missed in training. Lifting to failure too often in training can cause the lifter to become accustomed to missing lifts and this is probably the worst of habits to acquire. Attempting PRs over and over and missing them, even if they finally do make one, only teaches the lifter how to miss lifts, not make them without missing. Lifting to failure does not guarantee a faster road to success, but it could lead the lifter on a road to early stagnation. Consistency in the amount of weight handled and also the times in motion are the hallmarks of good training methods that will set a lifter on the road to faster and more consistent gains over the long haul.

The Back Squat

The back squat can be executed in several different variations, as regards to the position of the bar on the back, foot spacing and the depth of the squat itself. The bar should be as high on the back or upper torso as is comfortable for the lifter. The elbows will be pointed downward from start to finish of the lift. The elbows should be inside the grip. The upper torso should be as vertical as possible. There are minor style variations to the hand spacing and how the elbows behave during a back squat, but like most style variations their benefit cannot be quantified one way or the other. It would be somewhat strange to think the arms could deduce some advantage of motion with respect to the legs, hips and upper torso during a back squat. In order to be efficient it is important to eliminate all unnecessary motions.

The depth of the full squat depends on two things: 1) the amount of ankle and hip flexibility, and 2) the size or mass of the upper (hamstrings) and lower (calves) legs. Lifters with thin lower legs or less bulk making up the calf muscle can usually squat down into a lower position. The feet can be placed far enough apart for a lower depth to be reached also. If the knees do not extend past the top of the shoe laces, the lifter can get into a lower position. Possibly the best position is for the lifter's thighs to be just below parallel and the knees over the toes in the full squat position. Most style variations are imposed on lifters because of their physiology and flexibility, and the lifter will have to work within those parameters, in order to find the most efficient motion from which to progress from. For those lifters that have flexibility problems, they need to consult an expert in that field of study. It's unfortunate but some people are sometimes not suited for the sport they chose, but are more suited for other sports, because of unfavorable physiological restrictions. Sometimes these restrictions are self imposed, such as lifters not gaining the necessary bulk for their height vs. weight class.

The downward motion in the back squat should be controlled and the upward motion should be 1 second or faster. When doing reps the downward motion should be controlled, but generally the same time in motion going down as recovering the squat. A fast piston like motion, when the weight is light enough to achieve that type of action. The back squat can be trained at different depths in order to work the sticking point area. There are three different depths; 1) Just above parallel, but only a small amount, 2) parallel, and 3) just a small bit below parallel or full. These sticking point areas must be developed to where the lifter does not ever experience deceleration during the recovery, with or without a timed rebound. It is probably not necessary to do a complete full back squat, if the lifter uses a timed rebound in the recovery of the clean. Some attempt at a timed rebound should always be executed regardless of the depth of the back squat. The change in direction from around parallel should be a smooth, but quick action for the purpose of overcoming the sticking point and for the drive in the jerk, as well as for the liftoff the platform.

Note: For some lifters progress can be achieved by doing half squats and others need to do full squats. Some lifters only do front squats and some only back squats. The debate about whether a particular type of squat hurts the knees is only relevant for each individual lifter. It depends on the lifter's physiology as to whether a particular type of squat is injurious to them.

Transitional Speed (Time in Motion)

One way to work the squats and pulls is to move as fast as possible with the lighter weights by doing sets of reps in a rapid fire piston like motion, being mindful to maintain form. Speed or faster times in motion have to be developed from the lighter weights up and not the heavy weights down. The only way a lifter can move faster is when the amount of weight is reduced enough to allow for faster times in motion. As the lighter weight's time in motion becomes faster, then the 1 second PR weight will almost automatically increase. Remembering, the squats and pulls are assistance lifts and are there to assist their 1 second and .67 second times towards handling greater weights than their actual PRs are in the competition lifts.

Example: A lifter can back squat 200k in 1 second and can also do 190k x 3 in 1 second average time. In order to progress the 200k in 1 second the lifter should progress the 190k x 3 to .9 seconds. If the lifter does 190k x 3 in an average time of .9 seconds this lifter should be able to add 10k to the 200k and still maintain the 1 second recovery time with 210k. Squatting more weight slower will not give the lifter any indication of what they can lift or if they have actually made any progress or not.

Generally the same 10k per .1 seconds can be expected from the fastest times to around 1 second. This 10k is not a relative amount where a lifter with a 100k back squat only gets 5k compared to a lifter with a 200k back squat. Both, strangely enough, receive the same 10k increase per .1 seconds. This follows the same paradox where a 200k x 3 back squat is equal to about 210k x 1, and a 100k x 3 back squat is equal to 110k x 1. Both lifters receive the same 5k per additional rep increase regardless of the level the lifter has achieved. This only occurs where the times in motion are 1 second, because slower times could allow for greater deviations, but deviations that could be non-beneficial or difficult to equate with anything meaningful.

Squat Limitations

The squats should be limited to 125% of PR clean & jerk. This does two things; it reduces the possibility of overtraining, overloading and compression, and it allows for more energy to be used for training the snatch and clean & jerk, which are also limited to 85% for the majority of training.

Squat limitations also reduce the need to believe that only by increasing the squats, regardless of the time in motion, can the snatch and clean & jerk be increased. It should be noted that the squats are assistance lifts, and not to be trained like they were a powerlifting event. If any lift or exercise outside the snatch and clean & jerk are pushed by attempts at PRs on a regular basis, those lifts and exercises become events equal to the snatch and clean & jerk and thus begin to compete with the snatch and clean & jerk for time, energy and purpose. It would be like a discus thrower trying to train the long jump at the same level of intensity, thinking the farther he jumped the farther he would throw. Long jumping might be beneficial if trained at a lesser degree of intensity, but trained at the same level of intensity the discus throw could begin to show signs of mediocrity.

Limitations do not mean the lifter is being forced to do less. It means they can do more reps or volume and try and increase their squat velocity while training at 125% and less of clean & jerk PR. Although, 125% might not seem like much to lifters who train the squats using 2 to 3 second times in motion, but those additional 1 to 2 seconds of time can wreak havoc on the lifter's muscular and adrenaline systems, directly affecting the training of the snatch and clean & jerk for subsequent workouts, especially over long periods of time.

Example: A lifter has a clean & jerk meet PR of 175k and 125% x 175k = 218k for the back squat limitation. This will only work if the 218k can be achieved in 1 second, if slower than 1 second the limitation should be reduced to that number. If the lifter can squat 230k in 1 second the 125% limitation should still stand at 218k. The majority of the training will be between 175k and 218k depending on the number of reps and sets, but every rep should be 1 second or faster, in order to train the fast twitch fibers to respond to the bidirectional velocities needed for the snatch and clean & jerk. Remember, greater force is a result of greater acceleration on the same mass.

I constantly hear from lifters and coaches that the squats must be trained to failure in order to increase leg strength, however, strength cannot be defined as both slower velocities and faster velocities on the same mass. As the weight increases past what can be achieved in 1 second the velocity decreases as the mass increases, resulting in no additional benefit from that increase. The problem with squatting to failure, besides the damage it does to the mental and physical well being of the athlete, is that failure is reached as soon as the lifter begins to decelerate, which could be well before the final squat is missed. Progressing the snatch and clean & jerk is dependent on the velocity of the squats, not from the amount of weight that can be handled using slower velocities.

The same times in the squat should be equivalent to those in the pulls and competition lifts. The snatch and clean 1st and 2nd pull is after all just an upward squat, thus making it imperative that both the squats, pulls and those same parts in the snatch and clean & jerk are in agreement velocity wise.

1) Snatch to full extension .67 seconds and clean to full extension .67 seconds.

2) Snatch and clean pull to full extension = .67 seconds plus .33 seconds for the 3rd pull = 1 second.

3) Front squat at 110% of clean & jerk and back squat with 125% of clean & jerk weight is 1 second or faster.

4) Front or back squat from just above parallel .67 seconds with 100% PR for front squat and 125% of PR back squat.

The overall time in motion for the snatch and clean is 2.5 seconds, but optimally it would be 2 seconds: 1 second for the 1st, 2nd and 3rd pull and 1 second to stand up with the weight.

Section 8: The Snatch and Clean Pulls

Pulls are executed for the purpose of increasing the volume or repetition of motion as regards to the 1st and 2nd pull without having to go through a 3rd pull or pulling under the weight. The pulls should never degrade to the point of becoming a grinding slow poorly executed lift. The amount of weight handled in the pulls depends on the velocity of those pulls. The velocity of the pulls should be in equilibrium with the velocity of the snatch and clean & jerk, as mentioned before, which is .67 seconds.

The lifter should execute the snatch and clean pulls to full extension the exact same way as they pull during the snatch and clean & jerk, regardless of the amount of weight on the bar. The arms should never be used to forcefully pull the weight upward. The lifter can go up on the toes and shrug the shoulders, but the arms should be forced to stay straight or ride out the momentum, without any stress placed on the arms. Remember the arms do not bend until the lifter is pulling under the weight during the 3rd pull and only for the purpose of pulling downward where less stress is being placed on the arms and shoulders.

The amount of weight should be carefully chosen that will allow each rep in each set to be executed at a consistent time in motion. When doing reps with weights in excess of the lifter's snatch or clean & jerk PR, the weight should be let down quickly to the platform and the lifter should reposition themselves for subsequent reps. In other words bouncing or touch and go motions off the platform should be avoided.

Straps create a mechanical advantage that cannot be transferred to the competition platform. The ability to overcome force or produce force cannot be developed through straps, because straps are not part of the human condition. Straps are for the protection of calluses, not for the purpose of aiding the lifter in moving more weight slower. Besides, since the pulls will be executed using around 100% of PR clean & jerk and snatch, no straps should be necessary.

Variations of the Pulls

1) Snatch and clean pull to full extension

The exact same mechanics used in the snatch and clean are used when doing the natch and clean pull to full extension. There are several ways to execute this type of pull. The lifter can go up on the toes and shrug the shoulders or stay flatfooted and shrug the shoulders or not. No forceful arm bending should occur regardless of whether the shoulders are shrugged or not. When timing the pulls to full extension the time starts when the bumper plates leave the platform and stops when the bar is pushed away from the midsection by the forward thrust of the hips.

2) Snatch pull with bar being placed at the midsection

The weight is pulled from the platform and the bar is directed into the lap or midsection with the knees kept back as far as possible. The upper torso is leaning forward and is not brought to vertical. The shoulders are pulled back at the top of the pull in order to pinch the scapula together as much as possible. The knees can also be locked to a straight leg position or some bend can be kept in the legs.

3) Clean Pull to mid thigh

The same mechanics as the snatch pull to the midsection, except the bar is pulled through only the 1st pull position and the knees are pulled back. The upper shoulders are also pulled back as in the snatch pull to the midsection.

4) Snatch and clean pull just below the knees

The bar is pulled to the knees with the knees being pulled back as much as possible.

When doing the snatch pulls to the midsection, or the snatch and clean pulls to the knees, the hips should be lower than normal so the legs can be used more to squat the weight up off the platform to the knees, thus eliminating the need for deficit pulls.

Snatch or clean high pulls should be avoided other than when warming up or when handling very light weights. The arms are not engaged until the lifter is pulling under the weight and there is no way to simulate a 3rd pull when doing pulls, because the wrist and elbows cannot be rotated to the catch position.

It can be claimed that doing snatches or cleans off boxes can bridge the gap between the 2nd and 3rd pull, but does it? If the 1st pull is eliminated it becomes easier to snatch or clean more off boxes right off the bat. Remember the 1st pull takes .5 seconds and the 2nd pull only .17 seconds. Besides lifting off boxes is different from lifting off the platform, so that is problematic in itself. As stated earlier the only real benefit to pulls is being able to snatch or clean pull a little more weight from the platform, and at the same time in motion that is achieved when doing the snatch and clean & jerk off the platform. Since pulling off boxes eliminates the 1st pull or at least most of the 1st pull, there is no way for the lifter to know their time to full extension would have been .67 seconds. In most cases achieving a snatch off boxes with straps will be 10k more than off the platform without straps. The time in motion of the 2nd pull will be .33 seconds or twice the time when pulling off the platform, because of the static start position off the boxes. The 3rd pull off boxes will be the same as when pulling off the platform. So there is no added advantage to pulling or lifting off boxes, and in my opinion, it's more of a disadvantage, since the lifter believes they can snatch the same off the platform that they can off the boxes with straps.

Section 9: The Competition Lifts

The snatch and the clean & jerk are the competition lifts. There are numerous volumes of books and videos detailing the technical aspects of these lifts. I hit on some of the points concerning the technique of these lifts earlier in the book. I suggest watching the top lifters in the world and study their every move at every position during the lifts and try and mimic their basic motions. They obviously do it right or they would not be the best in the world. Be mindful to watch the basic motions, the overall time in motion, and how low they receive the weight, and their footwork. Not their minor style variations, or idiosyncrasies so much.

It is greater precision and sustained velocities that makes it possible for lifters to advance to higher levels in the sport of weightlifting. It is always the worlds best lifters who possess the greatest technical proficiency and the greatest amount of strength developed through specific times in motion (velocity) over their competition at the time they become World or Olympic Champions. I believe that it is through the process of developing greater strength and specific velocities through precision that allows the lifter a greater latitude through which even more technical proficiency can be achieved.

The hardest part of training is not the workload or the hours upon hours spent in the pursuit of excellence, but it's the grueling conscious efforts that go into each and every lift and training session, as regards to precision, developing and maintaining specific times in motion and overcoming forces by using those specific times in motion. The most well thought out program in the world will not bear fruit, if the lifter is not patently aware of how precise, accurate and fast each and every lift has to be as they progress towards higher performances.

Nitpicking Technique

Most sports require an athlete to ingrain certain skill sets in order to perform all the basic motions required for that athlete to achieve in their sport to the best of their ability. In sports like baseball, basketball and football, split second decisions have to be made many times during a game. To the outside observer, those split second reactions give the appearance the athlete is consciously aware of those decisions. In reality, the athlete uses their unconscious mind to react to certain actions or situations during a game. The athlete's skill sets must be ingrained with precision, by executing similar plays or situations in practice and competition many times over. Once the athlete has to make a decision or make a reaction, there is usually not enough time for that message to go from the brain to the muscular system in order to react in time on a conscious level. If the athlete has not ingrained their skill sets to react in that split second, they will have to make a conscious effort, instead of unconscious. Conscious efforts can sometimes result in mistakes being made.

Conscious efforts can slow down maximal reaction time, because the muscular system must wait for the signal from the central nervous system, in order to react in time to that action or decision.

The more an athlete has ingrained all their mechanics of motion, with precision, the more they can use their unconscious to make split second decisions and reactions. The weightlifter is no different from any other athlete in this regard. But for the weightlifter, there are few if any decisions that have to be made during a lift, in fact, there is not enough time during a lift to make decisions. It takes about 1 second from the time the lifter begins the lift, and then catches it in the bottom position. For most sports reaction times are usually less than a second, and in many instances there is not enough time for the central nervous system to relay a response in time to the muscular system. In order for any athlete to react quick enough, they must rely on their ingrained skill sets and unconscious efforts to make a play or complete an event.

Again, the only way a lifter can know if they have pulled the weight correctly is: 1) if they do not have to jump back or forward more than usual, when catching the weight, 2) if they do not have to take steps forward or backward during the recovery, 3) the overall time in motion from the platform to standing up with the weight is 2.5 seconds or faster, and 4) the weight is received at the lowest possible trajectory point, i.e. full squat in the snatch and parallel in the clean, and just above parallel in the split jerk.

If one or more of the four elements stated above are executed incorrectly, then even if the lift is successful it will still not have been lifted with the amount of precision and/or time in motion necessary to develop full potential. These types of deviations in training should be counted as a missed lift for leaning purposes.

The myriad nitpicking of technique that can go on in weightlifting is endless and can cause paralysis by analysis to set in if this nitpicking goes on too long. From determining exacting angles of the joints, to where the shoulders and elbows should be placed before and during a lift, to where the weight should be distributed on the feet, does nothing to help a lifter. If a lifter has trouble with their technique and precision every time they make a lift, then they need to start over with lighter weights and iron out those problems before resuming training. It's not the coach's responsibility to keep having to teach the lifter how to lift, it's the coach's responsibility to teach them how to lift correctly the first time, so they don't have to keep nitpicking every lift.

What Do Repetitions Achieve

The subject of repetitions have been and are still a source of great debate among lifters, coaches and even sport scientist. There has never been a conclusive study done on whether repetitions are of value or to what extent that value is. What is true is that in a weightlifting meet the lifter is only allowed 3 single attempts in each lift. Outside of that it is obvious that repetitions are mostly geared toward a specific result. Bodybuilders are forced to do a tremendous number of sets of reps, but mostly in the 10 rep range per set. Powerlifters have many different routines which use various amounts of sets and reps in each of their events. They also are limited to one single attempt in competition.

High reps can cause the muscles to behave like a bodybuilder's muscles do when they begin to experience a large amount of blood flowing into the muscles. The pumped up effect causes the muscles to begin to shorten the extension. This also causes the lifts to become erratic, and the times in motion to degrade. This process must mostly be just endured as a means to get the lifter conditioned in order to begin the rigors of training.

Generally reps of 3 or more are for conditioning and singles and doubles are for increasing performance. It's not always about the amount of weight or reps per set handled as much as it is the volume of sets. Less reps would allow for higher levels of intensity and more reps would require less intensity and allow for more volume. Intensity vs. volume vs. velocity requires a good deal of experimentation and time in order to find out what works best for each lifter.

Paralyses by Analysis

The only time a lifter should ever miss a lift, is because there was too much weight on the bar. This can be easily corrected by lowering the weight. Continually having to analyze one's technical efficiency (style) can cause: "paralyses by analysis"; *a situation, so that a decision or action is never taken, in effect paralyzing the outcome.* This malady can come from three sources, the athlete's trainer or coach, a training partner(s), or directly from the lifter themselves.

Cause and effect refers to the philosophical concept of causality, in which an action will produce a certain response to the action in the form of another event.

There is never anything wrong with some analysis concerning a lifter's mechanics of motion, which adversely effect the path of the bar, if those motions are done too often, and are outside the realm of the lifter's own technical efficiency of style and posture, or outside their ability to correct themselves. It is expected of coaches to teach their lifters the proper mechanics of motion, and keep a watchful eye on their lifters. Errors should be corrected immediately, so they are held to a minimum. It is, however, impossible to be perfect all the time. Mistakes will happen occasionally, but when they do, they should not be addressed to the lifter's attention each and every time, unless they occur too frequently. At some point the lifter must themselves be aware of, and know why, they missed a lift and be able to correct those errors on their own.

Over analysis could destroy the confidence a lifter needs to perform well in training and competition. Constant analysis of every lift made or missed could also cause the lifter to be too much aware of those mistakes on a conscious level. The lifter's motor skills could be inadvertently slowed down as they consciously attempt to correct, in their mind, all the mistakes which were brought to their attention way too often.

Many mistakes lifters make are caused by an inability to produce the correct amount of velocity, and the lifter, at that point, has no control over those mistakes. Other times mistakes occur because of a certain amount of muscular fatigue in particular areas of the body. Sometimes the lifter is asked to lift more weight than they can handle with precision, and this will automatically cause errors or erratic lifting to begin. When this occurs there is no logic in pointing out mistakes, because the lifter has no control over their body with the amount of weight being handled to be able to achieve precise mechanics of motion. The weight should be reduced to where the lifter can execute the lift with precision, and then after precision is achieved the lifter can advance the weight.

The notion that lifters should never use "light weights" in training is absurd. It is not the amount of weight that is lifted, it is how the weight is lifted that is important, regardless of how much weight is loaded on the bar. Training is about precision and specific times in motion first and the amount of weight is secondary.

It is impossible to build precision with weights which are too heavy for the lifter to achieve precision with, or weights that cause erratic lifting to occur. It is far better on the athlete to progress from a point of precision than to try and progress by how much weight is lifted without concern for that precision. The same being true for specific times in motion, however, specific times should take precedence over precision, i.e., the lifter should not sacrifice those specific times for being more precise. Slowing down an action should never be the answer to problems concerning technique, since technique should include those specific times in motion.

Erratic lifting is when the lifter makes each lift different from the next, due to loss of balance, timing or catching the weight at different heights or having to take steps forward to secure the weight. Erratic style lifting is anything which is outside the lifters ability to achieve the lift with their exact technical proficiency.

The lifter should be told only once what mistake they are making, why they are making them and how those mistakes can be corrected. Otherwise, they will more than likely keep making the same mistakes. Simply pointing out mistakes is not enough information for the lifter to be able to correct those mistakes. This process of over analysis, due to the lifter handling weights which causes their form to break down, is what can cause a lifter to become paralyzed in their actions, as well as lose confidence in their own ability. A lifter should not be told what they are doing wrong, but should be shown how to do it correctly.

The Path or Trajectory of the Bar

The path or trajectory of the bar is generally a type of fingerprint for each lifter, and depends on the physiology of the lifter, and the proportionality of force production between the legs and back. A particular trajectory path cannot be changed once the lifter has ingrained their technical skills, but some change in the trajectory can be caused by imbalances in certain areas of the muscular system. Some minor changes can occur by changes in the minor elements, the foot spacing, and grip spacing, but basically the bidirectional motion from the knees to full extension cannot be changed because that is a reflection of the lifter's physiology and their own particular method of producing momentum.

Trajectory paths are only accurate to the point where the lifter's own skills are exactly proficient. Erratic lifting can cause small changes in the trajectory path. It is quiet difficult to determine what the best path should be for any particular lifter, based on inaccurate data, i.e., poor or inefficient technical skills.

If anything can truly be extracted from looking at a lifter's trajectory path, I don't know what that would be, or if it would even be of any useful benefit, other than it is what it is. The only useful benefit I can tell would be measuring the highest point of the trajectory to make sure it is the lowest possible point that the lifter needs to receive the weight. The lifter, however, should be able to sense how much the weight drops on them without having to measure it, and measuring it will not necessarily help the lifter to catch the weight lower or pull under the weight without over pulling it. It becomes a case where information can become useless, if there is nothing done about it. If a lifter jumps backward in the snatch a foot when catching it, the trajectory might show it, but it will not correct it or even tell the lifter if it needs to be corrected.

The Jerk

There are three basic styles associated with the jerk;

1) The Squat (power) Jerk
2) The Split Jerk
3) The Full Squat Jerk

The dip and drive are the exact same in the squat jerk, full squat jerk and split jerk. It's not until the bar leaves the shoulders that the feet begin to split apart during the split jerk or split apart laterally during the squat jerk. There is also a splat style, something between a split and squat. Both the full squat jerk and splat style are used by very few lifters because both are timing and balance intense. There are generally three variations as to how the feet are split apart in the split jerk.

1) The back thigh and knee being under the hips
2) The back knee being away from the hips but the back leg bent
3) The back leg being straight

The aforementioned styles are receiving positions which are used to catch and secure the weight. One is not particularly more efficient than the other, it mostly depends on the lifter's preference or which style is more efficient for them.

The most important aspect of the split jerk is the depth the lifter needs to go in order to secure the jerk as quickly as possible without the arms re-bending or pressing out. Most lifters catch the weight when the front leg is just above parallel or just below quarter squat. Just above parallel I would consider to be optimum for securing the jerk overhead as quickly as possible and avert re-bending the arms.

There are some that think the back foot comes down first before the front foot. The toe does come down first, but it is not ready to absorb the shock until the front foot has come down. The reason the back toe comes down first is because the ankle is flexed in the back foot, and the front foot is not. In reality both feet have to come down at the same time at full impact. The toe coming down first does not mean it's fully down or ready to absorb the shock of catching the weight.

The thigh of the front leg needs to be close to parallel upon receiving the weight, regardless of which split style is used. The lifter should be aware of warming up by using a close to parallel catch and not use a power split jerk or that motion might not become ingrained enough when the heavier lifts come up. Power split jerks cause many jerks to be missed or cause the elbows to re-bend or not lock out per the rules.

The shoulders are shrugged before the bar leaves the chest. This is a transitional phase and is also an automatic response which supersedes pushing under the bar. The preceding shrug or raising of the upper body girth before the bar leaves the shoulder is a gathering of forces phase in order to make the change in direction or separation as quick as possible.

Before the bar leaves the shoulders the head needs to go back so the bar will clear the chin and move in a vertical path overhead. Simply grazing the chin can kill the momentum from the drive, and does not always feel so good. Overly pulling the head back could cause the upper body to be pulled back also and that could change the bar path to a more backward position, thus causing a balance problem during recovery of the jerk or dropping the weight behind the lifter or the lifter having to take steps backward to secure the lift.

The driving of the bar off the shoulders and splitting the legs apart has to occur simultaneously. As both feet impact the platform the arms will still be bent and the lifter has to drive the upper body downward to lockout the arms fully and secure the weight, as stated by the rules. It will not be considered a press-out if the motion is continuous towards a locked-out position.

The drive velocity is developed through the squats, not from doing jerks out of the rack or off boxes. The jerk from the drive to locking out should be around .5 seconds or faster from the lowest trajectory of the dip to the highest trajectory point from the drive. It can be as slow as .6 seconds, but any slower and the weight could be missed or pressed out. A lifter can develop good drive speed by doing the front squat in .67 seconds from just above parallel or parallel with 100% of clean & jerk, or doing back squats with 125% of clean & jerk in .67 seconds from just above parallel. Drive velocity is a function of a specific velocity or time in motion that can be produced to move the weight sufficiently enough for a successful jerk, and 105% of clean & jerk would be ideal.

The amount of weight that can be jerked out of a rack bears no relationship to the amount that can be clean & jerked, just as the amount that can be cleaned bears no relationship to the amount that can be clean & jerked. The majority of training must go into the clean & jerk, squats and pulls, and not into the jerk out of the rack or clean without a jerk. On somewhat rare occasions seeing how much can be jerked out of the rack will do no harm, but there is never any reason to do cleans without a jerk, baring some type of injury. The clean & jerk is one event, not two, and it should never be trained as two separate events or thought of as such, or the two events could well become mediocre, thereby causing the clean & jerk to stagnate or decline.

The Vertical Sport

Weightlifting is a vertical sport, in that all the drive and recovery motions are vertical. This means the bar path should be vertical and that requires the bar to stay close to the body in the snatch and clean during the 1st and part of the 2nd pull, and vertical during the dip and drive of the weight in the jerk. The bar, during the 1st and 2nd pull should not come into contact with the body aside from a slight brush of the bar on the body, which will not cause the weight to decelerate. The bar must stay within millimeters of the shins and thighs during the 1st and 2nd pull. During the 3rd pull the lifter is leaning back away from the bar, and the trajectory is guided by the arms in a vertical path as the lifter lays back to begin the pull under the weight and drop into a full squat position to secure the weight overhead.

Keeping the bar in close to the body reduces the forces that have to be overcome during the 1st pull and increases the production of force during the 2nd pull and the transfer of momentum into the 3rd pull. Crudely put, the acceleration can be linked to the three phases of the pull as fast, faster and fastest. The closer the bar is to the lifter then less force has to be overcome and more force can be generated during the 2nd pull and even more can be generated to pull under the weight. However, these velocities must be constantly reenforced, they do not come naturally even when ingrained. Most of the time lifts are missed due to a lack of momentum, and not always due to a problem associated with technique, but again technique should include those specific times in motion that have already been discussed.

Locking Out the Arms

The human skeletal system is capable of supporting 545 kg. The most important aspect of the snatch and jerk is the ability of the lifter to be able to lock the arms out solidly with the weight overhead. This requires that the muscles in the shoulders and elbows be flexible. It is most advantageous for a lifter to be able to slightly hyper extend the elbow joint. But the elbows should at least be flexible enough so the lifter can attain a solid lock-out with the weight overhead, while allowing the arms to be kept as relaxed as possible. The lifter should allow the elbows to find their own angle of rotation and concentrate on attaining a sold lock-out before securing the bar overhead.

If the elbow(s) cannot be fully locked out the lifter should alert that situation to the judges by pointing at the elbow(s) before attempting the lift.

Overly hyper extended elbows can be a bit of a troubling affair as the lifter becomes more and more proficient. It is very difficult to hold a heavy snatch or jerk overhead for very long with hyper extended elbows. At some point the joints can give out and become dislocated. As stated before, some lifters are disadvantaged by their physiology and some are advantaged.

Section 10: Auxiliary Exercises

The definition of training and exercise are basically the same thing, so it depends on what a person is doing at the time that determines whether they are exercising or training. Jogging, dynamic stretching and calisthenics would be exercising if done for that purpose only, but if used in conjunction with a sport the exercises would become part of that training. If the volume and intensity of exercises outweigh the training of an event, then the athlete is no longer training, they are exercising.

Auxiliary exercises need to be categorized as to their importance, necessity and functional attributes with respect to individual sports where time, distance and weight lifted are measured. Two questions need to be ask with respect to auxiliary exercises; 1) Will the exercise help improve performance, and 2) How.

It becomes a fine line between exercising and training when too many auxiliary exercises are included into the mix with the athlete's main event. When auxiliary exercises are trained at the same level of intensity, frequency and/or volume as the primary lifts, then those auxiliary exercises can have a negative impact on the specific training for the sport.

Auxiliary exercises for weightlifters go back several decades, and there is nothing new under the sun with respect to these exercises. Any type of motion used with a barbell that is not a primary lift would be considered an auxiliary exercise.

A few basic auxiliary exercises are listed below;

Muscle Snatch
Hang Snatch or Clean
Sotts Press
Behind the Neck Press or Jerks
Squat Snatch
Close Grip Snatch
Snatch High Pull
Drop Snatch or Clean from Power Position
Straight Leg Pulls (RDLs)
Snatch Balance

The above is just a few exercises that should mainly be used for warmup purposes and never pushed beyond any efforts which are the same type of efforts the primary lifts require. Attempting to do maximal efforts (PRs) with auxiliary exercises changes the scope of those auxiliary exercise to an event equal to the primary lifts. If half the total training time is spent doing the primary lifts and the other half doing auxiliary exercises then the average monthly intensity of those auxiliary exercises should be far less than that of the primary lifts.

The squats and pulls are not auxiliary exercises, they are essential to the training of the competition lifts and equally as important as those competition lifts. Squats and pulls are true assistance lifts. Auxiliary exercises are a variation to the full movement and not a variation contained within those full movements.

Pushing certain auxiliary exercises to excessive levels creates other events the lifter must become proficient at and that can cause mediocrity to set in between those auxiliary exercises and the primary lifts.

Auxiliary exercises can be classified as;

Warmup Exercises
Warm-Down Exercises
Partial Motion Exercises
Flexibility Exercises
Stabilizing Exercises
Overhead Exercises

Almost any auxiliary lift can be used during the warmup and warm-down periods before and after training. The amount of weight used during these warmup or warm-down periods should not exceed effortless. Any auxiliary lift that is taken to something near maximal effort should be ordered first and during a session when the snatch and clean & jerk are not being trained.

Some of the partial Motion Exercises are listed below;

1) Snatch off Boxes (blocks)
2) Hang Snatch and Clean
3) Snatch and Clean from upright Position
4) Jerks out of a Rack (all types)
5) Cleans without a Jerk
6) Snatch Balance
7) Overhead Squats

Power snatches and clean & jerks should not be considered variations of the full movement and not an auxiliary exercise.

It should be noted that the above partial exercises cannot and must not ever exceed the volume and intensity of the training of the snatch and clean & jerk off the platform. It takes a tremendous number of repetitions over time to become good at anything and if the lifter wishes to set PRs in the muscle snatch then that effort alone will detract from the performance of the primary lifts. Auxiliary exercises should mainly be considered a means for including variations, increase the performance of the primary lifts and for periods of recovery or active rest. Auxiliary exercises should never be used to vary the training, because the training of the primary lifts must take precedence always.

Flexibility exercises would be anything that would promote better flexibility where needed. Forcing the upper torso to be more upright when doing squats needs to be accomplished with light weights, so a more upright position can be attained without the stress and tension of maximal weight.

Stabilizing exercises would include front and back quarter squats and jerk recoveries at different depths off boxes or inside a rack where such overloading can occur. The main thing is not to overload much more than what the lifter can actually back squat or jerk, unless the lifter is well conditioned to handle that type of overloading on the body. There should be a gradual increase in the intensity of the overloading and never a quick shock to the system. If the lifter has no problem with their stability then doing stability exercises might not be needed.

Overhead exercises would include the military press, push press, jerks out of a rack or off boxes in all variations. As the squats and pulls should never be grinding efforts (contain deceleration) the military press and push press should also not become grinding efforts. This would also include the bench press, if applicable. Again, if jerks out of the rack exceed the volume and intensity of the clean & jerk then over time the clean & jerk will suffer for it.

Note: The press, push press and power jerk are a subset to the primary lifts rather than auxiliary exercises. Behind the neck press or jerks are auxiliary exercises.

The answer to a weightlifter making consistent progress lies with the primary lifts, and how those lifts are ordered, the frequency, intensity, volume, the specific times in motion and precision of those lifts. A weightlifter's training cannot be coupled with a myriad of exercises, powerlifting type motions or bodybuilding exercises. There is not enough time for the weightlifter to become both an exercise fanatic, sculpt a body beautiful, or become a stunt lifter, and still find the time to train for the purpose of reaching their full potential as a weightlifter. The snatch and clean & jerk full movements contain all the auxiliary exercises mentioned above in some form or fashion. There is no need for redundancy within the system. The only backup the lifter has would be the squats and pulls, and the only events that need to be trained and pushed are the snatch and clean & jerk full movements. Auxiliary exercises on their own cannot and will not aid the lifter in reaching their full potential. Auxiliary exercises are mainly fillers for varying the training and for recovery or active rest periods as well as warming up and warming down. Auxiliary exercises are only useful when linked in the proper way with the primary lifts.

The snatch and clean can be broken down into partial lifts, but those partial lifts cannot be put back together as a full movement with the expectations of making that full movement more efficient. The clean should never be executed alone as a separate lift for any reason, other than some injury or fatigue that might keep the lifter from doing jerks for a while. The clean & jerk should not be viewed or trained as two separate lifts, but as one full movement. It is far easier to only clean a weight than it is to both clean and jerk the weight. Conventional wisdom says doing only cleans will help the jerk because more weight is lifted during the clean than when doing a clean & jerk. Yes, but it also leads to overloading and possibly overtraining of the clean itself and could have a negative impact on the clean & jerk over time.

Certain partial lifts, such as the drop snatch and clean, snatch balance and snatch and clean off boxes are most often used as drills or as some mechanism that will fix specific problems with a lifter's mechanics. Most of these so called drills will not fix any problems, because in most cases the problems needing to be fixed are excluded when doing such drills. Once the perceived problem is solved, the lifter will more than likely revert back to their original technique when the weight reaches a certain percentage of PR. Partial motions can only be ingrained as a partial motion, and cannot be transferred over to the full movement, because they are not the same. Partial movements are different from full movements, because they lack the transitional phases.

Learning how to lift in parts is not the most efficient way to learn how to lift. It is the fastest, but it leaves the lifter without being able to feel through the transitional phases contained in those partial lifts. A beginner should be shown how to do a snatch and clean & jerk and then they should try it as a full movement from the beginning, and work out whatever technical problems they encounter while continuing to do the full movement. They are going to encounter the same problems either way.

Another problem with doing partial motions, as a means to increase the velocity of the bidirectional motion, is they can't. Athletes are equipped from the beginning to be as fast as they will ever be. An 11 flat 100 meter runner is not likely to ever run a 10 flat 100 meter race, once they have fully developed. All the training and weight training in the world won't change that. Only the unidirectional motions contained in the squats and pulls can create a situation where more weight can be lifted, by maintaining those specific times in motion, using whatever inherent quickness the lifter already possess.

The muscles used when doing auxiliary exercises or partial motions are not used in the same way when doing the full movement. Doing the snatch or clean off boxes is not the same as doing those off the platform. The mechanics are different, the accelerated velocity is different and the trajectory is different.

Snatch squats are nothing more than a behind the neck jerk with a wide grip and then doing a full squat. The snatch squat has little or nothing to do with the snatch, where the weight has to go through a 1st, 2nd and 3rd pull, of which the snatch squat includes neither. If a lifter has trouble with their balance in the bottom of the snatch, doing something different like snatch squats will not and cannot fix the problem, because balance problems originate from the platform, and can only be fixed by doing the full movement using precision and specific times in motion.

All the auxiliary exercises and gimmick lifts in the world will not progress the lifter if the squats and pulls are not progressed in weight using specific times in motion. The clean & jerk will not progress if the squats and pulls are not increased by weight using specific times in motion and if the clean & jerk does not progress, neither will the snatch. Progress in the snatch must succeed the progress of the clean & jerk, and never precede it. Even if that means holding back the snatch until the clean & jerk is progressed in both the gym and in competition. This concept is extremely important unless the lifter wants to become a snatch specialist.

As mentioned before, the squats and pulls are not auxiliary exercises, they assist those velocities needed for the clean & jerk to progress. The unidirectional motion of the squats and pulls are used to maintain the progress of the clean & jerk. If those squats and pulls are trained as a means to the end they will begin to resemble powerlifting events or bodybuilding exercises regardless of the technique used. Simply calling the high bar squat a weightlifting type squat is not valid when those high bar squats are still being trained the same way as powerlifters train their low bar squats.

Jerks out of the rack are valid if the training weight is kept at around 85% or less of PR clean & jerk, and only rare attempts at single PRs are executed, and not to exceed

100% of clean & jerk PR. Even jerks out of the rack can be questioned as to their validity, since the drive velocity is developed from the squats and the technical precision of the jerk has to be developed from the clean & jerk.

An athlete cannot get good at what they do by doing something else, and if they do something else too much and too intense they will get good at that and not what they do. If a lifter gets proficient at doing snatches off boxes, then that becomes their event. If they get good at doing heavy slow grinding squats, that also becomes their event. If they get good at snatching more weight using straps then they will always need straps to snatch more weight. If a lifter gets very good at jerking a lot more weight out of a rack than they can clean & jerk they will get better at the jerk out of the rack than the clean & jerk. Athletes should not cheat or fool themselves into becoming more proficient at something else. There are no short cuts to success or new exercises waiting to be discovered. All the lifter has in their arsenal of weapons are the primary lifts. Doing snatches off boxes can aid the lifter in developing the 3rd pull when greater weight is used over their PR, however, this is mainly for elite lifters who understand that doing snatches off boxes will of itself not aid the full motion directly, because the 2nd pull cannot be duplicated exactly as it is achieved off the platform. The volume of snatches off boxes must also be far less than the volume of snatches off the platform. The disadvantages of using boxes can far outweigh the advantages, if the lifter is only doing those snatches off boxes to see how much weight they can lift, instead of working on precision and quickness during the 3rd pull. Great care must be taken when doing snatches off boxes so that lift does not become another event and cause the snatch itself to become mediocre. Cleans should never be executed off boxes, because there is not enough inertia from momentum to make a smooth and controlled catch and use the legs as shock absorbers. I would classify doing cleans off boxes as a somewhat risky endeavor, and possibly even somewhat irrelevant, i.e., it becomes little more than a front squat from a full squat position.

Attempting to push the jerk out of the rack to higher levels than 100% can adversely overload the muscular system, and disrupt subsequent clean & jerk sessions. The amount of weight handled in the jerk out of the rack needs to stay in close agreement to the clean & jerk and never excessively exceed it, even if the lifter could do more.

The so called muscle snatch should never be executed with anywhere near maximum loads. At which point it becomes more of a press with a wide grip and that can put too much stress on the arms and shoulders, which can also disrupt the training of the snatch and clean & jerk in subsequent sessions. The muscle snatch also puts stress on the wrists the heavier the weight gets and the higher it is turned over.

Note: The muscle snatch is actually a stiff legged snatch where the knees do not re-bend after they straighten out the first time. The heavier the load the lower the bar is received and eventually the weight has to be pressed out overhead. Pressing the weight overhead precludes it from being called a snatch of any kind.

Executing snatch high pulls with maximum effort weights also puts undue stress on the arms and shoulders and can disrupt subsequent training sessions. Many times these disruptions are unbeknown to the lifter, and cause bad days to follow, but those bad days are never associated with doing something they should not have been doing in the first place. They are usually not associated with anything done in previous workouts, because for all too many lifters every workout session is a new day and accumulated stresses from previous workouts are never taken into account.

By adding more events to the training sessions by way of auxiliary exercises, where those lifts are pushed to maximum effort, the lifter is creating a situation where the primary lifts will begin to become mediocre. It's not how long a lifter can train, it's how much efficient energy is available for that lifter to train on. Anyone can train long and hard if the sessions are less efficient overall. But it should be noted, that training should not resemble some aerobic session where multiple sets of reps are executed with many various lifts. Weightlifting is the opposite extreme of aerobics.

If a lifter is not making any substantial progress, yet training 2 to 3 hours a day, 6 days a week, they need to reassess their efforts. Sometimes training too long and too intense can cause the opposite effect or a negative return. The lifter must find out what lifts to do and how to do those lifts that will ultimately help them to continuously progress. Whatever lifts are included it should be a long term solution and not a short term placebo or included for the sole purpose of setting a PR.

Cause and effect must also be taken into consideration when selecting auxiliary exercises. Just because a lifter's snatch is progressing and they happen to be doing snatches off boxes and muscle snatches, does not mean those exercises are the direct or indirect cause of that progress in the snatch. The snatch is a fixed percentage of the clean & jerk, and if the clean & jerk progresses, then the snatch should follow at the same ratio. If the snatch is increased due to the inclusion of auxiliary exercises for the snatch, but the clean & jerk does not increase in proportion, then their might be too much emphasis being placed on the snatch instead of the clean & jerk. The auxiliary exercises for the snatch might well work, but at what cost to the overall training and proportionality of the primary lifts. Lifters should also be weary of certain exercises arising out of popularity. Many times these exercises come and go with the wind, and suck up valuable energy without producing any benefit.

What I am trying to convey is that any lifts outside the primary lifts are not as essential as some might believe them to be. The more lifts added to the mix and trained at the same level of intensity as the snatch and clean & jerk can create a situation whereby as more lifts are executed as PRs the more mediocre the primary lifts will become, which includes the snatch and clean & jerk. The lifter cannot become a decathlete of lifting and expect all those lifts to progress at the same rate of change as when only emphasizing the primary lifts. Attempting to train 10 lifts as primary lifts, will always cause those 10 lifts to be more mediocre on average than when only training the 6 primary lifts and their variations. In other words, training the hang clean at the same level of intensity as the clean & jerk will cause both the hang clean and clean & jerk to become less efficient, not more, and how efficient does the hang snatch or clean have to become in relation to the full movements. I don't believe that doing a partial motion can or will benefit the full movement, because those partial motions are illegal motions per the rules of the sport of weightlifting.

Below is a list of lifts which contain motions that would create an illegal motion during competition;

1) Muscle Snatch when pressed out
2) Hang Cleans or Snatches
3) Lifting off Boxes
4) Push Press or Press to Lockout
5) Jerks out of a rack
6) Cleans without a Jerk
7) Behind the neck Overhead Motions
8) Deficit Snatch or Clean off a Raised Platform
9) Drop Snatch or Clean from Power Position
10) Using Straps

There are motions that are executed in reps, where those reps would be illegal per the rules, but the motion is not, such as additional front squats or jerks after the clean. It's not a question of auxiliary exercises being beneficial, but whether they add or subtract from the progress of the primary lifts. If taken to extremes, such as setting PRs or handling near maximum efforts in certain auxiliary exercises, there is no question that it will at the least hinder the progress of the primary lifts. Due to the laws of mediocrity and diminishing returns, this must occur.

Again, I am not advocating the elimination of auxiliary exercises, just some moderation in their volume and intensity, so there is no disruption in the training of the primary lifts and that certain auxiliary exercises do not alter the transitional phases of the full movements. Clearly there is not enough research as to the effects of auxiliary exercises on the change to the muscular system with respect to increasing an athletic performance. Many auxiliary exercises fall into a category closer to that of bodybuilding or they are assumed to work due to cause and effect. The only way to test certain auxiliary exercises is to link their validity to an increase in performance. If no increase in performance is achieved after several months of doing any particular auxiliary exercise then drop the exercise and see what happens after a few months time. Being hooked on certain auxiliary exercises is not a good reason to be doing them. A better method is trial and error by keeping what works and discarding what does not work.

The lifter should also be weary of those who sell programming packages where lifts, reps and intensity levels are pulled out of a hat as a one size fits all guarantee to increase performance. Each individual lifter, on their own or with the aid of their coach, must determine what works best for them, as it pertains to the workload, and which auxiliary exercises should be ordered. No one lifter is the same as another and what works for one might not work for another. Progress should come rather gradually, but consistently over several years, and without plaguing injuries. If this is not occurring then the training is not working.

Variations of the Primary Lifts

As long as the snatch and clean & jerk are started off the platform any variation of the lift would not be considered an auxiliary exercise. Variations should take precedence over auxiliary exercises, and be used often enough to help the lifter become more mobile in their actions and to help avoid becoming stale.

Variations of Snatch and Clean & Jerk
1) Snatch without moving the feet outward or keeping the feet flat.
2) Clean grip or narrow grip snatch.
3) Catching the snatch at different depths other than the full squat.
4) Clean without moving the feet outward or keeping the feet flat.
5) Varying the clean and/or snatch grip.
6) Catching the clean at different depths other than the full squat depth.
7) Vary the overhead motion of the split style using push press, push jerk (power jerk) or even full squat jerks.

Variations of Squats and Pulls
1) Squat using various foot spacings.
2) Squat using various depths.
3) Pulls to mid thigh, full extension and to the knees.

As can readily be seen there are substantially fewer variations of the snatch and clean & jerk that can be achieved when lifting off the platform. Partial motions allow for an expanse of near endless exercises lumped into the category of auxiliary exercises which mostly exclude the 1st pull. Eliminating the 1st pull too often will come at the expense of the 2nd and 3rd pulls development.

The professional lifter, one who only has to lift weights for a living, are in a better position to add several auxiliary exercises to the fray, but the lifter who has to work another job for a living does not have the time or energy to do multiple auxiliary exercises and is best served by sticking to the primary lifts and their variations.

Section 11: Warmup Protocols

How much stretching, or if any stretching is needed at all before warming up with the empty bar, is a source for debate. I believe each individual lifter has to figure that one out for themselves, because I have no way of knowing how much or how long each individual lifter's muscular system needs to be stretched or warmed up before actual training can be commenced, and I doubt anyone else does either.

The process of going from the empty bar to the final top end weight, should be handled by making sure enough reps and sets of reps are executed that will ensure the lifter is fully prepared to begin increasing the weight incrementally. This again must be left up to each individual lifer, because some lifters take longer to warmup up than others and some lifters are clearly more flexible to begin with without stretching.

The weightlifter should do their warmup routine with the empty bar by doing similar or the same motions they will be doing when they begin their training. The lifter should stretch into the positions they will be executing slowly and deliberately.

The following lifts are what I consider to be warmup lifts where the empty bar is used. This list does not include the snatch or clean & jerk proper because those lifts are begun after the warmup has been completed with the empty bar and commenced with the loading of the first incremental weight where a full movement can take place with the correct height of the bar off the platform.

Power Snatch and Power Clean & jerk
Stiff Legged Snatch
Clean and Press and Behind the Neck Press
Muscle Snatch (stiff legged snatch) no press out
Drop Snatch / Snatch Balance
Squat Snatch or Overhead Squats
Back Squat and Front Squat
Stiff Leg DL
Good Mornings
Press from a Full Squat
Press with a Snatch Grip
Snatch Grip Press from a Full Squat
Side bends with the bar on the back
Side to Side Twists with the Bar on the Back

The above list of exercises, and there are tons more, should be part of the warmup routine with the empty bar at the beginning of the session, and can be repeated between exercises, but that is not always necessary. The lifter should design a warmup routine that suites their needs and stick with it as consistently as possible from workout to workout and including the competitions. Warming up with empty bar should not become an aerobics session, but just enough warming up to begin the incremental loading.

If the lifter normally starts with 60k in the snatch then there should be some warmups between the empty bar and 60k, so the 60k does not cause too much of a jolt to the muscular system. For lifters who have totals around 100k, it is best to add 2.5k incremental increases from the empty bar to the top end weight for that session. For totals around 200k, 5k incremental increases and totals around 300k or more, 10k incremental increases. There should be a gradual change in the amount of the incremental increase as the amount of weight the lifter is able to handle increases. There's quiet a difference between an open lifer starting with 60k who can snatch 150k, than a lifter starting with 60k who snatches 100k. The shock to the muscular system is considerably less, when starting with 60k, to the lifter who snatches 150k than the lifter who does 100k.

There are also issues concerning the incremental warmup increases with respect to ingraining motions and maintaining specific velocities for the remainder of the incremental increases that will get the lifter to their top end weight. Jumping quickly from the empty bar to the top end weight by taking only a couple of intermediate increases, will not create a smooth and consistent change in the muscular system or ingraining process. If those intermediate jumps are erratic and slower than normal they might well stay that way when handling the top end weights.

From the empty bar to the top end weight or last warmup lift during a meet the lifter might move at a somewhat slower velocity to full velocity and the catching of the weight might also go from a higher catch to the final lower full velocity catch. This can occur gradually as the weight is increased, as long as the lifter is patently aware of those changes in depth and velocity.

The warmup with the empty bar through the incremental increases to the top end weight should become a consistent routine during the training phase. The more consistent routines become the more the lifter can rely on the data collected from those sessions, and it should become easier to tell how and why progress was made or not made. Consistent lifting from one session to the next is one of the most important ingredients to the programming schedule. Consistency is important in both the amount of weight lifted and specific times in motion of those lifts, as well as the technical precision during the transitional phases of the lifts.

Section 12: Core Principles of Training

Core Principles are advisements which determine how certain aspects of training should be conducted, in order for that training to be consistently executed. The principles below are not in any particular order of one being more important than the another, but adhering to principles of training can be just as important as the programming, since programming only includes how much weight is to be handled and not how that weight is to be handled.

1) Arched back

The arched back is important for both leverage-ability during the pull and stability, during the catch and recovery, also for the dip and drive in the jerk and recovery from the jerk. It's not enough to just be able to arch the back, the lifter must strengthen the lower back muscles. This stability in the lower back can be accomplished by doing the squats and pulls with an arched back. As far as my own personal feelings are, the arch in the back is the most important position in lifting. It is not a basic element in lifting, but it is an essential style element for the purpose of developing efficient motions.

2) Execute controlled downward motions in the front and back squat.

In order to develop the legs as shock absorbers the downward motion should be a bit slower and controlled than the upward motion, i.e., no crash diving into the bottom of a squat. Controlled downward motions in the squats are beneficial for the drive in the jerk.

3) Execute squats at different depths.

This works the sticking point better than going the same depth all the time. It is also a way to vary the squats. A bit below parallel would be the optimal position for doing squats for receiving the weight in the clean. The main factor is that the change in direction be as quick as possible and not cause any form breakdowns or slower accelerated velocities. A little over quarter squat allows considerably more weight to be handled than at parallel or full, but regardless of the depth the change in direction should be as quick as possible.

4) The squats should be executed using a timed index of 1 second.

The 1 second time in motion correlates to the total time of the pull to full extension plus receiving the weight $(.67 + .33 = 1)$.

5) All front and back squat reps should be achieved in 1 second or less.

When doing reps the time in motion needs to stay consistent from one rep to the next and from one set to the next. If not then the weight needs to be dropped down so this can occur.

6) The competition lifts should be executed with maximum controllable velocity using an overall time in motion of 2.5 seconds or faster for maximal weights.

The overall times in motion in the snatch and clean (from the platform to standing up with the weight) should be executed with as much velocity as possible from the first warmup to top end weight (at least from 70% of PR) The time in motion of 2.5 seconds should not be allowed to get slower, but instead the weight should be reduced to maintain the 2.5 second overall time in motion.

7) The pulls to full extension should be timed at .67 seconds with 100% of PR snatch or clean & jerk weight.

The times in motion should be recorded and a monthly average calculated, so if those times creep up over .67 seconds, the lifter will be alerted to that fact, and some alterations in the programming can occur to correct the problem.

8) Minimal use of straps

Straps are an advantage to force production and accelerated velocity, and cannot be used in competition. Straps can be used occasionally in the snatch and when doing heavy pulls, if needed. Straps should never be used in the clean & jerk for any reason. Straps should be alternated in the snatch so the lifter does not get too accustomed to using them.

9) Lifting off boxes should never become a primary lift.

Executing snatches off boxes should never become as frequent or as intense as the snatch off the platform. The snatch off boxes should be a limited variation and a month before a meet lifting off boxes should be greatly reduced or eliminated.

10) Times in motion should be recorded, measured and discussed frequently.

11) The front and back squat out of the rack should mimic close to the exact same foot and grip spacing the lifter uses in their recovery from a clean & jerk.

Some slight variations in foot spacing will occur when taking the weight out of the rack, and this is to be expected. For the most part the foot spacing should be the same as the recovery stance and sometimes a wider stance can be used, on occasion, to help with mobility when the weight is received with a very wide stance.

12) The snatch should be trained at the same monthly average intensity percentage of PR as the clean & jerk or less, but never greater.

In order for the snatch and clean & jerk to stay in proportion or close to the 80% ratio of snatch to clean & jerk these lifts need to be trained at the same percentage, such as 80% of PR. The snatch should never be allowed to be trained at a higher percentage level (on an average monthly basis) than the clean & jerk. As the ratio of snatch to clean & jerk increases the clean & jerk will become stagnant and the lifter might be in jeopardy of becoming a snatch specialist. Far better to be a clean & jerk specialist, but keeping both lifts in proportion is preferred.

13) Missing lifts in training should be avoided as much as possible.

This principle is important for two reasons, the first is to instill some confidence in the lifter, and in their training, and the second is to ingrain the notion of not missing to the point where missing becomes a source of calm frustration and the lifter will do almost anything to not miss a lift during competition or training.

14) Always leave the gym knowing more weight could have been lifted.

This does not mean a lifter maxes out a lift and still believes they could do more. There has to be an actual feeling based on reality that more weight could have been achieved. This means leaving the gym without any misses, erratic lifting style and/or slower times in motion.

Training can be somewhat complex when adding in certain limitations on time in motion and precision lifting, but without those parameters established and ingrained it can be unknown as to how and why progress was achieved. Some lifters progress without regard for specific times in motion or precision, but they will never progress to full potential, because they will become stagnant before full potential is achieved or the times in motion become too slow, which eventually can impede progress.

Section 13: Training Systems

Training systems are wide ranging and various, and are based on coaching methodologies. Different coaches have different systems and methods so those systems are always in competition with other coaches systems. Programming and the methodology within a system should be planned by the coach or trainer and be agreed upon by the lifter.

A training program where sets and reps and percentages of PRs are used for individual lifts and exercises is not a system, those are routines within that system. What some lifters or coaches call a Bulgarian or Russian system are methodologies of how performance should be increased. Those methodologies are built around the frequency of training, the intensity of the training load over time, how the lifts are ordered and what lifts should be included in that system, the limitations on the squats and pulls and acceptable velocities of those squats and pulls, as well as the social behavior of the lifters within that system. Simply trying to achieve the same routines within the so called Bulgarian and Russian systems will not work, without an understanding of the methodology behind those systems, or, preferably, being trained under the coaches who created those systems, however, those systems are often times meant for lifters who have reached, or nearly reached, their full potential; sometimes called high performance lifters.

There is a big difference between lifters who have reached full potential and those that have not, as far as how training can be conducted. Lifters who have reached their full potential only have to maintain their squats and pulls, but lifters who have not reached their full potential need to continue to progress those squats and pulls. The main difference is there will have to be limitations set on the amount of weight to be handled in the snatch and clean & jerk while the squats and pulls are being progressed. For the lifter who has reached full potential there is less restriction on how much weight they can snatch or clean & jerk in training. It is far easier to maintain the squats and pulls than it is to increase their performance, especially using specific times in motion.

There are several elements which should be incorporated into a training system;

1) Consistency of the system.
2) Simplicity of the system.
3) Goal oriented system.
4) Periodic inclusions of recovery workouts to gain back performance.

Consistency of the System

Weightlifting requires the athlete to progress on a consistent and constant basis, and to progress as rapidly as possible. It is important to develop a system where all the functions of performance, specific velocities, timing and balance are contained within the lifts directed specifically for the purpose of competition. The primary lifts should be trained in a specific order and at specific limits of performance. The order of the primary lifts should not overly vary, so the lifter can establish goals, and record and monitor their progress. When various auxiliary lifts are introduced into the training system too often, and trained at too high a level of resistance, those auxiliary lifts become exceptions to the primary lifts and in most cases redundant to the primary lifts, and could take additional energy and time away from the lifter's training of the primary lifts. The primary lifts are necessary for the lifter to advance at a higher and faster rate, and to better prepare that lifter for the competitions. Auxiliary exercises should be kept at a level of resistance that will not interfere in the progress of the primary lifts, but will aid in that progress.

The idea of getting in shape is not something weightlifters discuss, as track & field and swimmers often do. To the weightlifter being in shape is synonymous with how much they can lift. While this is true in some respects the point of getting into shape is also a way to maintain a certain level of performance as well as progress that performance. If the lifter is not in shape for lifting or training they will experience more highs and lows and progress will be slowed or halted. Being in shape does not mean how much weight can be lifted on a periodic basis, but how much weight can be lifted in each session of training on a consistent basis.

The amount of weight handled in each session must also become consistent in both volume and intensity. There should be no large swings in percentages, such as from 60% to 100%. The working weights need to be limited so the squats and pulls can continue to progress under the conditions of specific times in motion.

Simplicity of a Training System

As there might be some underlying meaning to executing certain lifts in training that fall outside the realm of the sport, but additional lifts added to the fray must be carefully scrutinized as to their importance and necessity. Again the question must be ask as to the need for other types of exercises and why.

The snatch and clean & jerk should be scheduled almost every workout, although with some alternating of intensities. The squats and pulls should be alternated to some degree. This might seem tedious or mundane, but no more tedious or mundane than a runner, cyclist or swimmer's training is. Variations to the workouts should come through alternating the squats and pulls and manipulating the volume and intensity of the clean & jerk and snatch, and inclusions of certain and specific auxiliary exercises. The exact same motions for each lift should be executed every workout and the same specific times in motion should also me achieved. The times in motion in the squats can be varied by trying to move faster with lighter weight.

Auxiliary exercises should come after the primary lifts, and the weight should be somewhat effortless and never stressful or cause too much fatigue for subsequent workouts to be less efficiently performed. The greater the volume of auxiliary exercises becomes, then the overall level of intensity of those exercises should be reduced.

A word of caution; an athlete cannot get good at what they do by doing something else. The squats and pulls are not something else, they contain the same inherent motions as the snatch and clean & jerk. Snatches off boxes are something different as are muscle snatches or hang snatches or cleans. Using straps is something different. Doing something different is fine as long as it does not interfere in the progress of the primary lifts, alter the precision, does not create slower times in motion or disrupt the timing and balance of those primary lifts.

Goal Oriented System

Both long term and short term goals should be programmed into the training, but most of all the training should render consistent increases in the primary lifts from year to year until full potential is reached. The lifter should be aware if they are making progress, and if not they need to be ready to make the necessary adjustments to that training. The main goals should be increasing the meet PRs and not just the gym PRs.

Recovery Sessions

A well defined system should have certain periods of recovery included at periodic times. Recovery workouts are for the purpose of both rest and gaining performance from previously intense workloads, and after meets. There should be some time set aside after a major competition to rest without any athletic activity for up to two weeks. At the very least the lifter should only use very light weights (60% or less) during this time.

During the rigors of training some workouts will be more intense than others and the next workout might have to be tapered down a bit to account for the fatigue factor. In this case it's better to be safe than sorry. This will require some adjustment to be made to the schedule or the lifter can go by how they feel and keep the intensity down enough to recover for the next workout.

I have nothing much to say about things like cryotherapy, message, special drinks or supplements. These forms of recovery have never been proven through scientific research to aid lifters in their ability to physically recover from one workout to another. It takes rest to recover from being overtrained or even from overreaching. In most cases lifters just continue to push forward and have faith in these snake oil products and remedies until it's too late. Most injuries are due to fatigue or being over trained and all the cryotherapy and special drinks in the world will not and cannot keep a lifter from becoming over trained when they continually train too long, too hard and too intense too often. All anyone can do is leave these decisions up to the lifter, with one caveat; buyer beware.

Keeping the Competition Lifts the Main Events

The mindset of the lifter should be adapted to the notion that the competition lifts are the only events and all other lifts or exercises should not be allowed to become another event equal to or even close to equal to the training and disposition of volume and intensity levels as the competition lifts. The idea that by forceful pushing of the squats and pulls using a separate squat or pull routine will automatically increase the snatch and clean & jerk is unfounded. The only way the competition lifts can be increased is by training the competition lifts as the main, and only events, and augmenting that training using the squats and pulls, by keeping those squats and pulls velocity in agreement with the velocity of the competition lifts. Volume of pulls and squats should also be commensurate with the volume of snatches and clean & jerks. If the squats and pulls are trained as in powerlifting, or with slow and grinding velocities, those squats and pulls will fall outside the definition of assistance lifts and become another event, which will compete for the energy stores and adrenaline supplies needed for the competition lifts.

The law of mediocrity comes into play when too many lifts or exercises are pushed to maximum efforts (PRs) too often and as near as often as the snatch and clean & jerk are pushed. In other words, as more events are attempted to be made proficient, then the more mediocre each different event becomes. If the snatch, clean & jerk, squat and pulls are pushed continuously for greater weight in each lift then the efficiency of all 4 lifts will decline or the level of mediocrity among those 4 events will be an average of the total proficiency. If a decathlete could score 900 points per event, and decided to increase the efficiency of one event to 1,000 points then the other 9 events would lose part of the 100 points gained. In order to progress the decathlete has to progress each event equally. In weightlifting the primary lifts also have to progress through predefined measurements of performance and not just the amount of weight handled.

Performance Indicators

Indicators are lifts that when executed reveal to the lifter how much more they can do without having to do it.

Indicators can be faster times with a previous PR, or increases in the singles and doubles with more weight, but at the same specific velocity. Indicators must be tangible and real and not intangible, such as being over weight or using straps. Establishing a PR jerk out of the rack is not an indicator of what can be clean & jerked. Snatching more off boxes with or without straps is not an indicator of how much can be snatched off the platform. Doing something different cannot accurately be correlated to an increase in performance.

Performance indicators must come from the competition lifts primarily and indirectly from the squats and pulls. Increases in squats and pulls can be deceiving and are not always good indicators, unless those increases are consistent and are achieved with specific times in motion.

Example: A 200k back squat in 1 second is achieved in .9 seconds a month later. This does not always mean the lifter can do the same weight consistently in .9 seconds, so it takes longer to determine performance indicators with the squats or the pulls, until those lifts are consistently executed with more weight, 210k in 1 sec. or at the same time in motion with 200k in .9 seconds.

Consistency in the weight lifted is far more important than simply how much weight can be lifted as a one shot deal, where that amount of weight might not be achieved again in over a month or even a year. There are times when squat PRs come once a year, and that should be completely unacceptable. This normally occurs when the squats are executed in very slow times using grinding actions. These type of one shot deals are more stressful on the lifter's mind than their body. The mind remembers those stresses and will unconsciously find ways to avoid that same experience. It can take much longer to recover mentally from extreme overloading than it does to recover from it physically.

The Elements of a System

A system is created to program training, direct the progress of the lifter and prepare them for competition. During the time between meets there are four phases;

1) Recovery Phase
2) Training Phase
3) Peaking Phase
4) Tapering Phase

The above four phases are not cycles because they are dependent on the training for a meet at a specific future date in time. These four phases as a whole could be considered a training cycle between meets. A conditioning phase is also outside the realm of this cycle between meets. Conditioning would commence after long periods of inactivity.

1) The Recovery Phase
The recovery phase should last at least one or two weeks after a major meet. The level of resistance should be kept at 70% or below for each and every lift and exercise. The second week after the meet the intensity should be gradually built back up to normal levels over the course of 1 to 2 weeks or even a month or two. The recovery cycle's purpose is to gain back performance from the training

before the previous meet and the meet itself. Recovery workouts scattered throughout the training cycle serve a different function than the recovery phase after a meet. Recovery workouts are inserted into the mix as a mechanism to keep the lifter from becoming overtrained or excessively fatigued, which might cause subsequent workouts to become less efficient, due to erratic lifting or slower specific times in motion occurring.

2) The Training Phase
The training phase includes all training, except for the rest or recovery days and the peaking phase of about 1 or 2 months before a major meet. Beginners should enter as many meets as possible, until they reach a level where they can qualify for a national meet, after which they should train exclusively for that major competition and train through other meets, depending of course on the importance of those other meets.

Lifters who have reached a top level of performance and are being selected for international competition, will also have to pick the number of meets they enter, and train through those meets that are of less importance. The more meets a lifter enters and fully peaks for, will leave less time for training and making gains in the primary lifts, and periods of rest will also be lessened.

If a less important meet comes along, during the training phase, the lifter need not peak for it, just enter and compete, and then resume normal training after a few recovery sessions. It is best when training through a meet to plan on going 6 for 6 and reduce the 3rd attempts between 90% and 95%.

3) The Peaking Phase

The peaking phase is a transitional phase from the training phase, whereby the lifter hones in their skills and precision to exacting degrees with near maximal weights for the sole purpose of competition.

4) Tapering Phase

Tapering normally occurs about one week out through a reduction in percentage of PR and reduced volume.

Recovery Phase Workouts

Many times right after a weightlifting meet the lifter will actually feel more energetic in the first two weeks following that meet, especially if they have fully peaked for that meet. It is not uncommon for the lifter to set PRs in the gym during this time which are equal to or even greater than those achieved in the meet. On the surface this might seem like a good thing, but in reality it can cause the lifter to overload their muscular and adrenaline systems, thereby making subsequent workouts less effective.

It is advisable to cut back after a meet for one or two weeks or longer and enter a period of recovery, by handling 60% or less of PR in all the lifts executed in training. This will allow the muscular and adrenaline systems and other bodily systems to recuperate from the rigors of the peaking phase and from the meet itself, and gradually begin building back up those systems over the course of the subsequent training sessions.

The number of reps and amount of weight should be reduced during the recovery phase the week after a meet.

Other aspects concerning fatigue or minor soreness should also be taken into account. Some meets might require the lifter to take off from lifting for two weeks or longer, and/or reduce the levels of intensity even more.

Section 14: Linking the Primary Lifts

Linking: To bind or link certain elements together into an interconnected whole
for a specific purpose or benefit.

Linkage between the primary lifts can be accomplished in three ways;

1) By Velocity
2) By Technique
3) By Incremental Increase

Linking the Snatch to the Snatch Pull

By velocity means that the 1st and 2nd pull in the snatch, which comprises the pull from the platform to full extension, be the same velocity when doing snatch pulls to full extension. If the pull to full extension is .67 seconds when doing 80% to 100% in the snatch then it should also be .67 seconds when doing the snatch pulls with the same percentages between 80% and 100%.

By technique means the 1st and 2nd pull in both the snatch and snatch pull be executed exactly the same way without any deviations whatsoever, including the approach to the bar and the set up.

By incremental increase means the snatch pulls should be commenced where the snatch left off and then worked up from there to the top end weight for that session, but should not be slower than .67 seconds when going over 100% of snatch PR or deviate from the snatch technique.

Linking the Clean & Jerk to the Clean Pull

By velocity means that the 1st and 2nd pull in the clean, which comprises the pull from the platform to full extension, be the same velocity when doing clean pulls to full extension. If the pull to full extension is .67 seconds when doing the clean & jerk with 80% to 100%, then it should also be .67 seconds when doing the clean pulls with the same percentages or more.

By technique means the 1st and 2nd pull in both the clean & jerk and clean pull be executed exactly the same way without any deviations whatsoever. In other words a powerlifting type dead lift cannot be linked the same as a clean pull.

By incremental increase means the clean pulls should be commenced where the clean & jerk left off and then worked up from there to the top end weight for that session, but not slower than 1 second when going over 100% of clean PR or deviate from the snatch technique.

Linking the Front Squat to the Clean & Jerk

By velocity means that the recovery in the front squat be the same velocity as when recovering from a clean. Both the front squat at 110% of clean & jerk PR and clean recovery should be 1 second or faster or .67 seconds from just above parallel.

By technique means the recovery from the front squat must be exactly the same as the recovery from the clean & jerk without any deviations. The hand and foot spacing should be exactly the same when standing up in the front squat as when standing up after the clean.

By incremental increase means the front squat should be commenced approximately where the clean & jerk leaves off and then worked up from there to the top end weight for that session, but not to exceed the 1 second time or deviate from the clean & jerk recovery technique.

Linking the Snatch and C&J to the Squats and Pulls

By velocity means that both the snatch and clean from the platform to standing up with the weight should take from 2 to 2.5 seconds and not be slower than 2.5 seconds. Within that 2.5 seconds the recovery time should be 1 second or faster and the pull to full extension should be .67 seconds. The 2 to 2.5 seconds is generally the same time during the downward and upward motion in the squats.

The technique and incremental increases remain the same as described above for each of the primary lifts.

Linking the Back Squat to the Clean & Jerk

By velocity means that the recovery in the clean be the same velocity as when doing the back squat. If the clean recovery is 1 second when doing the clean & jerk then it should be 1 second when doing the back squat, regardless of the weight.

By technique would primarily include the foot spacing and keeping the back arched and as upright as possible. Technique should be at least consistent and done the exact same way each time when doing the back squat so the back squat can be progressed as fast as possible.

Linking the Snatch to the Clean & Jerk

The velocity must be maximal in both lifts and the technique varies due to the nature of the two lifts. The lifter normally maintains a certain ratio between their snatch and clean & jerk and that is what needs to be linked. This means both the snatch and clean & jerk should be trained at the same percentage of PR on an average monthly basis, and the snatch should not be allowed to become a greater percentage of PR than the clean & jerk. The snatch can be the same or less, but never greater.

Snatch and Clean Pull Variations

Snatch and clean pull variations, such as pulls to mid thigh or doing just the 1st pull are assistance lifts for the pulls and still qualify as a linking element. In the case of the pulls to mid thigh the hips are positioned lower than normal so more of the legs can be used to lift the weight off the platform to the knees and/or 1st pull position. Velocity should be close to .5 seconds for the 1st pull.

Different Depths in the Squats

Going to different depths in the squats is also a variation if the difference in depth is a departure from the depth most consistently used. Different depths can be achieved during a set of reps or separately. The three basic depths would be;

1) Just Above Parallel
2) Parallel
3) Full or Just Below Parallel

Non-Linking Elements

1) Attempting maximal squats and pulls, and still using specific times in motion, or any attempts at personal records during training cannot be linked, but might affirm the lifter's training is working. Linking requires consistency from workout to workout, and does not include one shot PRs, no matter how significant those might appear to be.

2) Moving slower deliberately in the downward motion of the squats and pulls has little or no benefit as a variation to those squats and pulls. Slow is never a good thing when it comes to athletics, and thus moving slow on purpose is antagonistic to the lifting motions. Remember, strength is defined by a faster change in acceleration against a given mass. If the lifter uses slow grinding squats and pulls (dead lifts) and slow 1st pull and slow grinding clean recoveries then the primary lifts will become linked in that way. It does not mean the lifter will not reach a decent level in the sport, it just means they will never reach their full potential or have any hope of becoming a top lifter in the world. Slower velocities reduce the chance of a lifter reaching their full potential.

3) Erratic or non precise motions cannot be linked even if the time in motion is adequate. Some imprecision is necessary so the lifter can learn to make split second adjustments when things don't go exactly as expected, but for the majority of training erratic motions should be held to a minimum and nearly eliminated when handling 85% or less.

4) If the top end weights vary too much that cannot be linked. Only a consistent amount of weight can be linked. It is far better to go to 80% every workout than vary the percentage by going from 70% to 100%. Somewhere between 70% to 85% is optimum for keeping the primary lifts linked together. This does not include the practice meets, parts of the peaking phase or the meets, but primarily the training phase.

5) Auxiliary exercises cannot be linked. Partial motions break the link in the chain at some point, such as hang snatches and cleans, snatch and cleans off boxes, jerks out of the rack, cleans without jerks, overhead squats, etc., If the link is broken the lifter is exercising not training. Nothing wrong with some exercising as long as those exercises do not become events or primary lifts.

Once all the primary lifts are linked and training is focused on maintaining those links, the lifter should progress as fast as possible to full potential. The volume and frequency of the snatch and clean & jerk serves to get the lifter into shape rather than being a linking element. More frequency and more volume is needed in the competition lifts and less frequency and less volume in the squats and pulls. The squats and pulls are there to assist the specific velocities of the competition lifts, not to overshadow or replace those competition lifts as the main events.

Note: The phrase "getting strong" is usually in reference to increasing a lift by the amount of weight only and not by increasing that weight using a constant time index (TI). In most cases the lifter is not actually getting stronger, but getting slower.

Achieving maximal velocity in the competition lifts is more important than achieving precision. It is through the attempt at maximal velocity that the lifter can eventually come to be able to control that velocity and link that velocity to their precision where continued progress can be achieved up to full potential.

Section 15: The Training Phase

There is a stark difference between going into the gym to train for competition and going into the gym to set personal records (PRs), especially for the beginner or any lifter that has not reached their full potential. It might seem like the only way to make progress, that will ultimately lead to full potential, is to constantly be going for snatch, clean & jerk, squat and pull PRs, but it only seems that way.

Since full potential cannot be quantified as to it's actual meaning, it must be determined by what the lifter wishes to achieve at their peak level of performance. This should be part of the long term goal setting parameters, and be within the confines of their own situational reality or lifestyle. It would be a bit presumptive of any lifter to think they could become a world champion by holding down a full time job or being married and raising children. Their goals should be confined to becoming state or possibly national champion. Their full potential would be those lifts that would make it possible for them to compete for a national championship title over a 4 to 5 year period.

Certain auxiliary exercises that incorporate parts of the full movement contained in the snatch and/or clean & jerk are still a snatch and clean & jerk. There is no fundamental difference in a hang snatch or hang clean, or a snatch or clean off boxes and the snatch and clean & jerk itself. The difference is that the partial lifts, which also at times include cleans only and jerks out of the rack, leave out the transitional phases that are needed for the lifter to become proficient at a high level of performance. Leaving out those transitional phases is what causes partial lifts to be classified as doing something different.

Auxiliary exercises can be beneficial if not trained at the same level of intensity as the snatch or clean & jerk, but trained at a reduced level of intensity so as not to interfere in the precision and velocity of those transitional phases of the competition lifts themselves.

The squats and pulls are not auxiliary exercises, but are assistance lifts for the snatch and clean & jerk where those bidirectional motions (2nd and 3rd pull and the jerk drive) are being assisted through an increase in those unidirectional motions of the squats and pulls. It is possible to develop perfect technique, yet not progress to full potential or to any level, because through the unidirectional motions of the squats and pulls (1st pull) is where greater forces can be overcome to allow the lifter to produce sufficient force (bidirectional motions) to make the weight.

The beginning lifter must become proficient in the competition lifts and the squats and pulls at the same time. The squats and pulls are a continuation of the incremental increases after the clean & jerk. It does little good in the long run to squat or pull without doing those squats and/or pulls after the clean & jerk or snatch so the incremental increase can continue upward toward the top end weights that will be used in those squats and pulls. This gives the lifter some understanding of the difference they have between those squats and pulls and their clean & jerk. That difference being mainly in the time in motion of those squats and pulls.

When using times in motion, such as 1 or .67 seconds for the recovery and .67 seconds for the pull to full extension, the difference between the squats and pulls and clean & jerk will allow for more accurate data to determine correlations. It should be remembered that there are no meaningful correlations with respect to maximum slow grinding or decelerating squats and pulls.

The lifter should snatch and clean & jerk first in training and manipulate the volume and intensity whereby the squats and pulls can be continuously progressed up to full potential. Attempting to train the snatch and clean & jerk at too high a level of intensity and/or volume can and most likely will defer the squats and pulls progression. Once the squats and pulls go into a long period of non progression, the snatch and clean & jerk will become stagnant, regardless of the volume and intensity or use of auxiliary exercises used to increase the performance of those competition lifts.

Progress of the squats and pulls has to be defined by the amount of weight increasing while the velocity stays constant or an absolute amount of weight tied to a fixed amount of velocity. In other words, increasing the squat from 200k to 220k is not an actual PR if the time in motion was 1 sec. for the 200k, but 1.5 sec. for the 220k. An actual PR or benchmark, due to those restrictions on velocity, would mean the 220k would have to be achieved in 1 second also. Although Squat PRs are not a vital statistic for progressing the snatch and clean & jerk, they do serve as an indicator.

There is a percentage of PR value at which point the lifter begins to show signs of form or posture breakdowns. It's where the lifter can control their motions and the weight does not control the lifter. It is where the possibility of missing a lift is reduced to near zero. It is where greater concentration can take place on a conscious level without the lifter's velocity slowing down. It is where maximum velocity and precision can take place regardless of how the lifter feels. This is where a maximal weight can be lifted a maximal number of times per month. This percentage is what allows the lifters who have not reached full potential to progress their squats and pulls unhampered toward full potential. That percentage is 85%.

The training weight for the snatch and clean & jerk should not exceed 85% when doing reps or multiple sets of singles. The average monthly intensity for both lifts should be 80% and the highest percentage reached at any one time during a training month should be no more than 90%. It should be noted that if 85% feels like 100% then there is something wrong with the lifter. Either they are fatigued or over trained from previous workouts and the 85% should be reduced to take that into account.

Full potential is where every ounce of proficiency in the competition lifts and squats and pulls has been squeezed out of the lifter and there is nothing left to increase performance. At this point the lifter hopefully has become stagnant at a high level of performance and can maintain that high level of performance for several years or until the aging process overtakes them. Becoming stagnant is not a bad thing if the lifter has reached their full potential. It is a bad thing if stagnation occurs before reaching that full potential. The only way to keep from becoming stagnant early on in one's lifting career is not to allow that to happen. The only way to keep it from happening is to limit the snatch and clean & jerk to 80% average monthly intensity while the squats and pulls progress and limit the times in motion of the snatch and clean to 2.5 seconds or faster. Limits on the squats of 110% for the front squat and 125% for the back squat should also be in place.

Some might suggest that the snatch and clean & jerk are like throwing the discus or shot put or sprinting, but far from it. The discus thrower and shot putter do not have to deal with an ever increasing implement, and the sprinter does not have deal with the additional incremental loading on their body from one qualifying heat to the next. Another difference in weightlifting and the throwers in track & field is the throwers do not have to catch their implement once they have released it. They only have to deal with a bidirectional motion that does not incorporate radical changes in direction or overcoming greater forces, only the production of force through that straight line bidirectional motion. Throwers, high jumpers and long jumpers gradually build up momentum to be unleashed through torque and/or leverage.

Track & field athletes can spend enormous amounts of time practicing their skills for their events with less concern of fatigue or overtraining setting in compared to the weightlifter. It is simply not rationale to think a weightlifter can train like a thrower or sprinter and that training not effect subsequent sessions in a negative way. The accumulation of stress and fatigue is followed by an involuntary reduction in performance, and lower levels of intensity. This occurs when both the competition lifts and squats and pulls are equally pushed at 100% efforts for too long.

The only way to stave off this involuntary reduction in performance is to limit the amount of weight to be handled in the competition lifts during the training phase, and only allow those working weight limits to increase as the squats and pulls increase. Once the lifter reaches full potential they are no longer bound by the same principles as those that have not reached full potential.

The essence of the Bulgarian, Russian, Chinese, Kazakhstan and now the Iranian systems are based on bringing lifters into those systems that have reached or nearly reached their full potential. Any lifter who attempts to use these types of systems and have not reached their full potential will become stagnant very early on. These systems are designed for the purpose of getting all they can out of those fully developed lifters until their performance declines. The same way any professional athlete is used in other team sports. Drugs also play a large role in how long and hard a lifter can train, but at present there has been such a crackdown on drug usage that it would behove any lifter to train drug free.

Programming a lifter's training is not a system or a philosophy. Programming is a set of directives that if followed will lead to a result which neither the coach or lifter can be sure of. It is and always will be the lifter's responsibility to progress themselves. What is more important than programming is the philosophy or methodology of the system and some assurance that a particular system will allow the lifter to achieve their full potential. The system must produce results past what the lifter can even imagine in order for that system to be viable. No two lifters are alike so each system will have to be micro managed for each individual lifter.

Pushing for technical proficiency in the snatch and clean & jerk is only a viable solution if the squats and pulls continue to progress. Only through the development of the squats and pulls used to overcome greater forces and allow the production of greater force and momentum does technical proficiency occur. Without velocity built into the squats and pulls it matters little how technically proficient a lifter becomes. That proficiency is not relegated to just the snatch or clean & jerk and the myriad of auxiliary exercises, it must also be tied into the squats and pulls to exacting degrees, even more exacting than the competition lifts themselves in some respects. The squats and pulls cannot be progressed efficiently outside the confines of the motions included in the competition lifts, because the ratio of lift to squat decreases as the technical efficiency of those squats decreases.

It's not a question of the lifter engaging in short periods of so called strength cycles, the lifter must always be in a strength cycle in order to reach full potential. The only way to achieve this is to limit the intensity of the competition lifts and therefore the volume can be increased, i.e., the number of singles or doubles, at least to a point where that volume does not begin to interfere in the progression of the squats and pulls.

All the lifter has to do is make sure they do not decelerate during the recovery of the squats or during the 1st pull. When they feel they are starting to decelerate, the squats and pulls should be halted at that weight and the weight reduced to finish the desired number of sets. The lifter over time should ingrain those feelings or measure the actual time it takes to recover a squat or execute the pull to full extension. The squats and pulls can only be pushed to higher levels of proficiency by not decelerating. Grinding efforts do not help the lifter get through the sticking point, it only makes the sticking point more difficult to get through.

Over time the longer the lifter uses slow grinding actions in the squats and pulls that will cause the lifter to reach stagnation quicker, because there is less room to progress the slower those squats and pulls become. A lifter can squat and pull more weight by moving slower because the force is decreased as the mass increases due to the slower changes in acceleration. Therefore moving more weight slower is not as efficient as moving the same weight faster. The lifter is not stronger, just slower, and the muscular development is switched from the fast twitch fibers to the slow twitch fibers. It's the fast twitch fibers that are needed for the snatch and clean & jerk's 1st pull and recovery. It's the 1st pull and recovery that allows the lifter to move at their optimum accelerated velocity during the 2nd and 3rd pull. The 2nd and 3rd pull cannot be made faster, those bidirectional motions are inherent in each lifter and other athletes as well. The more force the lifter can overcome during the 1st pull will mean more force can be generated during the 2nd and 3rd pull, but only up to the inherent ability of the lifter to produce those optimum bidirectional motions.

Lifting off boxes will not make the lifter faster during the 2nd and 3rd pull, as often advertised. It might make them more aware of the velocity they need to achieve after the 1st pull, but it will not and cannot make a fully developed athlete faster. The ability to produce force and momentum is specific to each lifter and there are no exercises that can cause the lifter to become faster than they already are. The squats and pulls are not designed to directly increase the acceleration during the 2nd and 3rd pull, but are designed to indirectly cause the 2nd and 3rd pull to become less burdened by gravitational forces on the lifter, thus allowing the lifter to be able to move at their inherent optimum velocity more efficiently during the 2nd and 3rd pull, i.e., at .17 seconds and .33 seconds.

The developmental stages of the athlete hinges on their ability to fully develop their skills along with some sort of weight or strength training regimen. Even those throwers in track & field at some point reach their full potential before they bow out of the sport. The throwers in track & field have the same problem as the weightlifter. If the throwers become stagnant in the squats and pulls before they reach full potential in those lifts, that will have a direct impact on their ability to progress their event to it's full measure. Accelerated velocity is just as important to the throwers as regards to the squats and pulls as that velocity they attempt to generate during their throws. Those bidirectional motions are dependent on the velocity that can be produced within those squats and pulls. It makes little difference how much weight a thrower can squat or pull if those velocities are not in close agreement to those velocities used in their event.

The actual training for the weightlifter should not become so complex that the complexity overshadows the underlying objective, which is to continually progress the squats and pulls and competition lifts while maintaining those specific times in motion. Auxiliary exercises are simply derived from the primary lifts, and their usefulness cannot be quantified so readily, apart from that underlying objective. It can only be assumed that certain auxiliary exercises are beneficial, however, there is no assumption that need be made with respect to the squats and pulls, they must continue to progress regardless of what else the lifter does with respect to training. Also, the argument is not whether auxiliary exercises are viable, but whether they are a benefit to the goals of each lifter.

The objective of training is not only to prepare the lifter for competition, but to allow that lifter to develop their full potential. The competition lifts and auxiliary exercises associated with those competition lifts must not be allowed to stymie the progress of the primary lifts. They must be held to the minimum level of intensity and volume that will keep the primary lifts' progressing until full potential is reached. This might even curtail the lifter's ability to perform at peak performance levels in meets for several years, which would be a tradeoff between being a decent lifter or a world champion.

Once the lifter reaches a certain age, they only have a short period of time to reach full potential. It must happen rather quickly, if it is to happen at all. Full potential is usually reached over a period of five years, but once started it cannot be halted or it will never happen. Fully developed means the lifter has stopped growing and has reached puberty or around 17 years of age. That means the lifter, regardless of what they achieved before the age of 17 has 4 to 5 years to reach their full potential or 21 to 22 years of age, if training has been consistently applied over those 4 or 5 years. Past this period of 4 to 5 years progress can normally only be achieved by moving up to another weight class.

The following is a list of conditions that could cause a lifter to become stagnant before reaching full potential;

1) Slow, grinding squats which cause the lifter to decelerate during the sticking point.
2) Slow grinding pulls where the lifter loses posture and/or decelerates during the 1st pull.
3) Not allowing the squats and pulls to be brought up gradually using specific velocities over the time it t takes to reach full potential.
4) Training the snatch and clean & jerk at too often and too high a level of average monthly intensity.
5) Adding too many auxiliary exercises to the mix where too much energy is taken away for the squats and pulls to continuously progress, thereby creating diminishing returns.
6) Training longer and harder past what is needed to make gains.
7) Going for gym PRs too often in the primary lifts or other auxiliary exercises.
8) Fully peaking for too many meets a year instead of training through enough meets to allow the squats and

pulls to continue to progress, being more prepared for the major meets.

9) Using straps when no straps are needed.

In order to keep the competition lifts honed in, while the squats and pulls are progressing, will take some manipulation as regards to all the primary lifts. The snatch and clean & jerk should be trained at the average monthly level of intensity of 70% to 85% before the peaking phase of a major meet. The back squat and clean pull are generally free to be pushed, but staying within those parameters of specific velocity of 1 second for the squats and .67 seconds for the pulls. One reason we rarely hear of how much the top lifters in the world can squat or pull is because they never attempt those types of squats and pulls that cause deceleration to occur.

Limits can be established on the squats and pulls to make sure the lifter does not venture into the area of deceleration. For the back squat a limit of 125% of clean & jerk can be set up, whereby the lifter never exceeds the 125%. The front squat could be limited to 110%, the clean pull to 125% and snatch pull to 110%. Some limits need to be established so the lifter does not decelerate during any rep or set of reps and there is no unnecessary overloading on the muscular system.

There is no reason to increase the intensity of the clean & jerk or snatch to over 85% that often. Training is not just about biology of the human system, but it's also about physics, and in my opinion the physics plays a much larger role in training than does the biological systems of the lifter, because the physics can be observed and measured. Biological systems are harder to interpret.

The volume of squats and pulls and the levels of intensity have to also be monitored and manipulated in order to keep those squats and pulls progressing. It's a relatively slow process and it cannot be rushed, because the competition lifts are still the main event and must be trained just as diligently and carefully and with a greater amount of volume than the squats and pulls. So it becomes a very delicate matter to progress the primary lifts as one unit, especially when those primary lifts are not linked properly. Running into the gym and banging away at PRs all the time in the competition lifts and squats and pulls and particular auxiliary exercises might work for a while, but at some point the hammer will drop and the progress will slow or become halted. Full potential cannot be achieved in this manner, it is impossible. The lifter needs to hold back their temptations for attempting PRs in the gym, until full potential has been reached. PRs achieved in the gym should come by happenstance or not at all.

Becoming a national champion in some countries is not that difficult to achieve, and can often times be done without reaching anywhere near full potential. These methods are nothing more than common sense, not rocket science, and nothing in the way of complex programming is needed. All that is needed is a lot of patience and the lifter knowing their body and how they feel and what they can and can't do on any particular day or in any session, coupled with some limitations on the weight and times in motion of the lifts.

The backward approach to setting goals is to announce that one wishes to increase the snatch from 90k to 100k in 3 months. The problem with this type of goal is the snatch is dependent on the clean & jerk progressing, and the clean & jerk is dependent on the squats and pulls progressing. It is incorrect to set goals in the snatch or the clean & jerk without first establishing the goals needed in the squats and pulls. How can those goals in the snatch or clean & jerk be achieved, if the squats and pulls are not achieved in concert with the snatch and clean & jerk progress.

The volume of snatches should be greater than the volume of clean & jerks so the snatch will serve as a conduit to get the lifter in shape to sustain a 100% effort in the snatch in the meet and have the energy left over to also sustain a 100% effort in the clean & jerk.

The idea or purpose of the 80% monthly average level of intensity is to help the lifter recover faster from one workout to the next, because a 90% snatch day will have to be reduced the next workout to 70% in order to maintain that 80% average.

It should become very apparent to the lifter or coach if the squats and pulls are not progressing. The volume might need to be adjusted in the snatch and/or clean & jerk, or the volume and/or intensity in the squats and pulls might have to be adjusted. There is an ongoing battle raging between the competition lifts and the squats and pulls, and between the squats and pulls themselves. All these lifts are competing for the lifters energy stores and fatigue and overtraining is the enemy. The enemy can be defeated by limiting the intensity of the snatch and clean & jerk, or at least it can be kept in check as much as possible.

One might say, the snatch and clean & jerk intensity levels have nothing to do with the squats and pulls. It might seem that way, but the lifter has to understand that with every snatch and clean there is a pull and a squat. The higher the level of intensity the snatch and clean & jerk are pushed, then less energy is available for the squats and pulls. If the squats are scheduled first, then that will cause an automatic reduction in intensity of the snatch and clean & jerk. Squatting first is usually achieved during morning sessions, but if the squats are ordered first then the snatch and clean & jerk should be reduced to allow for precision and velocity requirements.

During competition, it is important to establish a good rhythm from one attempt to the next. Starting attempts should never be missed, and the second attempt should always be less than the lifter's meet PR. Only the third attempt in both the snatch and clean & jerk should be attempts at PRs. The first two attempts in both the snatch and clean & jerk should be almost automatic and less stressful, both mentally and physically to the lifter. A lifter should always make their first two attempts in the snatch and clean & jerk, regardless of what the outcome of the third attempt is. As regards to the 3rd attempt in the snatch, if it be a PR, it must be almost assured and take less effort than the 3rd attempt clean & jerk. Pie in the sky 3rd attempts are rarely if ever achieved.

Human beings are creatures of habit, and if the lifter is constantly going 2 for 6 or 3 for 6 in weightlifting meets they will ingrain that pattern and it will become difficult to get away from it, and get into the habit of going 4 for 6 or 6 for 6 in meets. How well or poorly a lifter does in a meet is directly related to how well or poorly they trained or prepared for a meet. Going to failure in training by attempting too many PRs in the gym will directly effect how that lifter performs in a meet. A lifter can just as easily ingrain a pattern of missing lifts in training as they can ingrain a pattern of not missing lifts in training.

Training Phase Programming

Programming is secondary to the methodology that will be the basis for the programming. Without a sound methodology the programming will be of little value. Linking of the primary lifts through specific times forms the basis of that methodology which can be incorporated into the programming. Limitations on the the squats and pulls and manipulation of the volume are other methodologies that should be considered when writing a program.

Order of the Lifts

The order of the primary lifts in a workout session is important for the purpose of getting the lifter into shape and allowing the progress of the squats and pulls to follow the competition lifts. Obviously the snatch comes before the clean & jerk and in most of the major sessions the squats come after the clean & jerk, as would the pulls. In lesser sessions the squats can come first before the snatch and clean & jerk. There is more allowance for variations in the lighter sessions.

Adjustments to volume and intensity should be programmed into the workouts when the lifter trains more than 1 session per day. It's never how long a lifter can train, but it's how well they can maintain their precision and specific velocities in each and every rep and exercise in every session.

Athletes get good at what they do by doing what they do, not by doing something different. It takes thousands of reps even tens of thousands to become exacting and proficient and to maintain and progress within that proficiency. Thus, training needs to be very similar from workout to workout. Drills and exercise variations cannot be quantified as to their benefit, only assumed because something done all the time cannot be extracted out of the equation to find out if the same results could have been obtained without doing them. Whether certain auxiliary exercises are useful or not can only be determined by the lifter or their coach through experimentation.

Repetitions, Frequency and Variations

Again the number of reps the frequency of the exercise and the number of auxiliary exercises are all based on how well the lifter can maintain their precision and specific velocity throughout their lifting career. There are no "bad days" only those workouts where the lifter has been forced into a reduced level of intensity due to fatigue or being overtrained due to previous sessions being too intense. These so called good and bad days need to be leveled out to where each workout feels about the same and can be achieved without misses, erratic lifting or slower times in motion.

In order to keep the training as simple and efficient as possible, primarily singles and doubles should be executed as regards to the primary lifts. Doing things like 5 sets of 5 in the squats and pulls is fine during a conditioning phase, but doing 5 sets of 5 in the squats will have a negative impact on subsequent training sessions during a training and peaking phase, depending on the intensity level of those 5 sets of 5. Since the squats and pulls need to be linked to the competition lifts, and are assistance lifts, those squats and pulls should follow similar repetition methods used in the snatch and clean & jerk.

Incremental Increases

The amount of incremental increase from one lift to the next will depend on what level a lifter has achieved. Generally the following increases are usually taken;

Snatch and Clean
1) Youth or beginners: 2.5k increases where the total is 100k or less.
2) Open intermediate lifters: 5k increases where the total is 100k to 200k.
3) Open Elite lifters: 10k increases where the total is over 200k.

There are variations to these increases and even top lifters might only take 5k increases to get in more volume through the incremental increases up to the top end weight. Generally it's not a good idea to take too large an increase as this can shock the muscular system and decrease the efficiency of the workout as a whole.

Squats and Pulls

1) Youth or beginners: 2.5k increases where the back squat is around 100k.

2) Open intermediate lifters: 5k increases where the back squat is around 150k.

3) Open Elite lifters: 10k increases where the back squat is around 200k or more. There can be variations to these increases and even top lifters might only take 5k increases to get in more volume.

Determining Working Weights for the Squats

There is no limit to how much weight can be handled for a single or double, in the squats, as long as the time in motion is 1 second. The snatch and clean & jerk are limited in weight so the 2.5 second overall time can be maintained, and the squats should be limited by a percentage of clean & jerk or 125% of clean & jerk as long as that 125% can be achieved in 1 second. The working weights will fall inside the 125% limitation. The limitation of the front squat should be 110%, as long as the 110% can be achieved in 1 second.

Limitations on weight are so the lifter does not excessively overload or become somewhat fatigued for subsequent workouts. On occasion during the training phase the lifter can attempt a maximal 1 second squat which might be over the 125% limitation. This is fine as long as it does not become to often and the lifter is confident they can make the lift in 1second or faster. Being mindful, the squats should not become another event by going for maximal efforts too often.

If a lifter's PR back squat in 1 second is 180k, then they will be able to do 170k in .9 sec., 160k in .8 sec. and 150k in .7 seconds (jerk drive velocity). When manipulating the intensity between 150k and 180k these times in motion should be achieved, so even though the weight has been reduced in a particular training session, the consistency of the maximal back squat is maintained as far as the equivalent times are concerned. If these times cannot be maintained then the weight should be reduced further and the number of sets completed. Once the 150k has been achieved in .6 seconds or 160k is achieved in .7 seconds, this would be an indication that the 180k could be achieved in .9 seconds and a new single PR could be attempted when the opportunity arose. But again the means to the end is to increase the velocity of the squats and not see how much can be handled as a 1RM.

The working weight for the front squat is figured the same as the back squat, although there has to be some alternating between the back and front squat as regards to volume and intensity. Both lifts cannot be progressed at the same time if both are trained at a high level of intensity. One squat has to be backed off for the other to progress. In most cases the front squat can be the sacrificial lamb, since front squats are achieved in the clean & jerk, then the front squat out of the rack can be reduced in intensity and volume and increased in velocity. There are some top world lifters that don't execute front squats, for varying reasons, and only do back squats. This is okay because they do the front squat during the clean & jerks.

Determining Working Weights for the Pulls

The lifter also has to ingrain the .67 second pull to full extension in order to determine what the top end weight should be for any particular session. There are three key times in motion during the pull to full extension. To just below the kneecap in .33 seconds, to the 1st pull (before the knees are pushed forward) should be about .5 seconds and to full extension should be .67 seconds. As long as these times are maintained there is no limit to how much can be pulled during any workout.

The only difference between a snatch pull and clean pull is the width of the grip. Without the 3rd pull involved the snatch pull is basically a clean pull with a wide grip. Generally the ratio of snatch pull to clean pull is approximately 85%. Doing snatch pulls after the snatch and before the clean & jerk could disrupt the clean & jerk workout, so I suggest doing snatch pulls after the clean & jerk, unless those snatch pulls are not going to be excessively voluminous or highly intense.

The amount that can be pulled regardless of velocity can be staggering. It can also be extremely stressful to the muscular system and adrenaline system if pulled incorrectly by bowing the back or grinding out the lift (decelerating). The single maximal effort in the snatch and clean pull should never be attempted or need not ever be attempted. What the lifter needs is for the snatch and clean pull to be at least 100% of snatch or clean & jerk PR, and for those pulls to be .67 seconds to full extension.

Note: Without a 3rd pull during the snatch and clean pull to full extension the weight will float at the point of full extension, because there is no 3rd pull. In this case, the time from the platform to full extension should be measured to the point where the weight begins to move away from the midsection or the upper torso is vertical. This might not give an exact time, but it will create a point of of reference for all those pulls.

The lifter should generally go by how they feel, as far as being able to maintain their precision and specific times in motion. Thinking that a lifter will do less work if they go by how they feel is absurd. Feelings are there to help prevent athletes from overreaching, overloading or overtraining. Telling an athlete not to use their feelings is like telling someone to touch a hot stove and then pretend it didn't burn them.

Hierarchy of Performance in the Training Phase

Specific velocities are the most important element in training, even above precision, since precision should be developed using specific velocities. In the beginning holding to precision and attempting to move as fast as possible is difficult to achieve, but over time that precision and specific velocity will become ingrained effectively.

Velocity or time in motion

a. Snatch and Clean: Approximately 2.5 seconds or faster.
In order for the snatch and clean to be executed at the most efficient level an overall time in motion from the platform

to standing up with the weight should be 2.5 seconds or faster. The slower the overall time in motion becomes then less available force production can be used to progress the lifter.

The snatch and clean have to have a certain value or optimum time in motion established from which to progress that motion from. This follows the same principle as the 1 second squats; the slower the time, then less force is produced on the same mass.

1) 1st pull is about .5 seconds
2) 2nd pull is about .17 seconds (to full extension)
3) 3rd Pull (from full extension to receiving the weight) .33 seconds
4) Standing up should be 1 second or faster

Above we have a 2 to 1 ratio of 1st and 2nd pull to 3rd pull, and a 2 to 1 ratio of 3rd pull to 2nd pull, but only if all the times in motion are achieved as such. Any change in those times will change the overall time in motion. Obviously the lighter the weight the easier it will be to achieve the 2 second time in motion, and as the weight approaches maximum efforts those overall times will slow down, but should never become slower than 2.5 seconds. Slower than 2.5 seconds is an indicator the lifter is decelerating during the 1st pull and standing-up, which can indicate the squats and pulls are being trained using slow and grinding actions (deceleration) during certain phases of those lifts.

b. Squats approximately 1 second or faster.
The 1 second squat is a general performance goal, but slower times up to 1.3 seconds are acceptable if they are

not counted as a PR in 1 second. When doing reps those reps should be executed in rapid succession and at the same time in motion. Squats from parallel should be around .67 seconds for the liftoff and jerk drive.

c. Snatch and clean pull: Approximately .67 seconds from the platform to full extension.
Each rep in the pulls should be reset as fast as possible and not bounced off the platform. The weight can be released after full extension or let back down under control for a dead stop reset.

Times in motion should be somewhat consistent during all sets of reps in the squats and pulls and snatch and clean & jerk, if the times begin to degrade too much then drop the weight down to the previous set.

Time in Motion vs. m/s

Generally m/s (meters per second) is used for research purposes, however there is a difference between using time and speed for training purposes. Time in motion is the same for all lifters regardless of stature, i.e., a 6 foot 6 inch tall lifter must pull the weight to full extension in .67 seconds the same as a lifter who is only 5 foot 3 inches tall. The m/s will be faster for the taller lifter, therefore using meters per second is a bit cumbersome compared to using time in motion. Another example would be track runners and swimmers use lap times instead of velocity for training purposes, therefore I believe the stopwatch (video measurements) should also be used in the training of a weightlifter.

Precision Training

In training never take a step forward in the snatch, if the lift cannot be saved by running forward dump the weight and continue the reps. Once the feet are reengaged back to the platform that is where they stay regardless of a make or miss. Stepping out or running out from under a weight uses up too much energy and causes additional stress to the joints. When doing power jerks or full squat jerks, if the weight is too far forward to keep from stepping out, dump it and continue on, being aware of the adjustment to the pull that has to be made for the next rep(s) to be achieved without any step outs. This process will make the lifter fully aware of their technical error and become more focused in subsequent sets. Dumping the weight instead of stepping out to save the lift, does not constitute a missed lift for training purposes. The same work was achieved, and a greater awareness of the pulling technique is gained, but only as long as the lifter does not continue to have to dump the weight, otherwise the weight needs to be reduced so they do not take steps forward.

The Amount of Weight

The amount of weight is not as important as the times in motion and precision. If the times in motion and/or precision begin to degrade, drop the weight down to the previous weight in the session and work back up. Also, volume or the number of sets of reps are more important than the amount of weight being handled during the training phase. The snatch and pulls require more volume relative to the clean & jerk and squats.

Maxing Once a Week

If the lifter maxis out both lifts every weekend that requires a train down of at least 2 previous workouts and a recovery period of at least 2 workouts after the max weekend. This leaves less time from week to week to train properly for the meets. As stated before, lifting to max in both the competition lifts and squats and pulls is a fast track toward stagnation, overtraining or even injury. Maxing out one lift every two weeks should be sufficient and still keep the average level of intensity at 80%. Also, anything over 90% should be considered maxing out during the training phase.

Number of Sets in the Competition Lifts

The number of sets executed in the snatch and clean & jerk should basically follow the same incremental increases as will be achieved during the warmup for the meet.
There are two types of incremental set progressions.

1) Wave Progression
2) Linear Progression

The wave progression is a corrective method used to reduce the weight down a few sets when things go wrong while going toward the top end weights. If the lifter misses a lift or starts becoming erratic they should go back a few sets and start over. There is no validity to doing the wave on purpose. The same volume can be achieved in the linear method. Besides, in meets the lifter never does wave progressions in the warmup room. Doing down sets should not be considered as a wave progression.

The linear progression method is the method most used and follows the same general incremental increases as will be achieved in warming up during a competition.

Section 16: Methodology

Most top athletes from individual sports achieve on their own, because a coach or trainer can only progress a lifter or athlete to the level of knowledge they posses or ability they once possessed, both usually being the same. The athlete must be able to assimilate and sort information and collect data as regards to training, and know what to do with that data. Coaches can be helpful but the lifter has to know if that coach is being helpful or not. The coach cannot lift the weight for the lifter and so the coach should not ever come to believe they know everything or they are the solution for a particular lifter. Coaches for the most part are at best there to advise and motivate the athlete, not control the athlete's every move and social behavior like a dictator. Athletes who need to be dictated to or motivated should be in team sports not individual sports.

Methodology

Methodology has to do with how the lifter will be executing their lifts in training, not how many reps or days of training will be scheduled. Using specific times in motion for the primary lifts is a methodology, as is training using precision (perfect motions repeated). Using slow grinding actions is a different methodology, usually encouraged by strength coaches who believe that time in motion is not relevant to a particular increase in mass.

Programming

All your dreams can come true if you buy the right program of numbers and percentages, well maybe not. The problem with programming is that is all that it is, numbers and percentages. Unfortunately programming is a necessary evil in all sports, however, simply going through a program, in and of itself, will not and cannot guarantee results. Programming should be predicated on specific methods and principles in order to be valid. For example, a squat routine without the particulars of the velocity of those squats is useless to the weightlifter. Doing 5 sets of 5 with 90% means absolutely nothing without knowing the velocity of those squats, how long to rest between sets and the allowance within that program to back off if the velocity begins to degrade during the set. Programming can never be much more than a general guideline and not something written in stone that must be obeyed at all costs. Developing a system through a methodology is more important than the programming. Programming should come from that methodology.

During the training phase the lifter will be averaging 80% using various sets of reps, but staying close to the same incremental increases that will be used for the warmups during the competition. Mostly singles and doubles when training the snatch and clean & jerk.

During the peaking phase the lifter will train the snatch and clean & jerk at 90% to 95% once a week, but not both lifts at the same time. The lifter should taper a week out from 85% down to 70%. Mostly singles during the peaking phase, but some doubles can be beneficial during this time, up to about 75%.

The squats should be limited to a certain percentage of lift, such as 110% of clean & jerk for the front squat and 125% of clean & jerk for the back squat. Making sure the 1 second recovery time can be achieved with those limits. The pulls should be trained at 100% of PR and at .67 seconds to full extension.

The volume of snatches should be greater than the volume of clean & jerks. The volume of squats should be the same as the clean & jerk, the volume of clean pulls should be less than the clean & jerk and the volume of snatch pulls the same as the volume of clean pulls.

Video and measure the times of all the top lifts in every session to make sure those times are staying consistent from workout to workout, and month to month.

Programming is often thought of as how many sets of reps or singles should be achieved with top end weights. However, the incremental warmups must be part of that programming and should be closely associated with the same incremental warmups that will be executed in the competitions.

Reducing the Weight Back to a Previous Set;

1) When a lift is missed.
2) When step outs occur standing up.
3) When the times in motion are slower (deceleration occurs).

4) When erratic lifting occurs other than slower times or step outs.

Athletes should not be bound, tooth and nail, by their workout program's suggested working weight that is scheduled. When problems arise, concerning missed lifts, fatigue, technical errors, imprecision or other reasons that might cause the lifter to not be able to perform up to par, then some reduction in the planned or scheduled amount of weight should occur. In the training phase the amount of weight is not as important as the volume or the consistency of times in motion and precision. If problems arise then a reduction in the weight is more beneficial than a reduction in the volume. There is no shame in reducing the weight down to a few previous sets and start over in an attempt to achieve those lifts with better precision or velocity. It is foolish to continue to attempt a weight that has caused a lack of velocity and/or precision to occur. The lifter should learn how to back off in order to fight another day.

Programming by the Numbers

The number of variations within a program can be staggering. There are hundreds of different types of sets of rep(s) configurations. It is impossible for anyone to know which combinations will give the best results. Programming for an individual lifter can best be achieved, in my opinion, through trial and error. Some lifters do better when they do more doubles or even triples than singles and visa versa. Some lifters might do better by squatting or pulling to maximum efforts without regard to velocity, even though they can reach a decent level they can never reach their full potential. Some lifters have more fast twitch fibers than slow twitch and are not able to train as long as someone with more slow twitch fibers or they might need more rest between sets. It takes time for the lifter or their coach to come to understand those characteristics in order to be able to devise a workable program.

I could bang out a bunch of numbers with sets and reps and which lifts to do on what day, but it would be completely meaningless unless several individuals could use it to their advantage. The odds would be considerably great against finding even one person. In other words there is no one size fits all program, but the methodology can be similar, i.e., the Europeans emphasize velocity in the squats and in the US more weight using slower times is preferred and in China some of both methods are used with a little more emphasis on velocity. In other words, following a so called Bulgarian or Russian system will do little good if the methodology of those systems are not followed.

Weightlifting does not require a strict type of programming. Of all individual sports only the runners in track & field, swimmers in competitive swimming, speed skaters and gymnast require some formalized strict programming schedule, and this does not include the sprinters in track and swimming. Weightlifting training is more akin to the throwing events in track & field and sprinting events in track and swimming, where several throws or sprints per workout at maximal effort are executed. These events along with weightlifting require a less rigid programming where the athlete can go by feel and in a strict rigid program the athlete is unable to do so, because they are constantly trying to get in shape. The weightlifter gets in shape through a less restricted program due to the constant watch on becoming overtrained. If the weightlifter's programming contains too much volume and is too rigid and strict then that will have an adverse effect on subsequent workouts, which could reduce the intensity level involuntarily, without the lifter knowing it and causing what is called a bad day. The lifter should never try and train through a bad day, but immediately reduce the volume and intensity or do some light auxiliary exercises or skip the workout.

It does not take a rocket scientist to devise a weightlifting program, as long as the methodology is known and the system established from that methodology is understood; simply plug in the numbers and see what happens through experimentation. Many lifters don't even use a program, they basically go into the gym and see how much they can snatch or clean & jerk or squat or dead lift and going to failure is their guide, of course this is not training, but it's competing, and trying to compete every workout might get a lifter to a decent level, but it will also get them to stagnation very quickly and well before they ever are able to achieve their full potential in the sport.

What is needed are programming guidelines that can help keep the lifter from becoming overtrained while allowing full potential to be achieved. The following program schedule will show how to manipulate the different elements that have to be dealt with on a month to month basis, but first a couple of terms need to be defined;

Average Monthly Intensity (AMI)

In each workout the lifter will achieve their maximal, not always maximum, weight in each lift (primary lifts only, since auxiliary exercises should never be executed to maximum effort). These maximal efforts are added up on a monthly basis and divided by the number of days a particular lift was executed, thus calculating the average intensity for that particular month. The volume can be noted on the schedule, but does not play a part in calculating the AMI.

Top End Weight (TEW)

The top end weight is simply the singular most weight lifted during a particular lift regardless of the sets or reps. Percentages can also be used or calculated afterwards.

Example: A lifter with a 120k snatch and 150k clean & jerk programs the snatch at 100k x 5 x 1 and the clean & jerk 130k x 3 x 2, then the top end weights are 100k and 130k regardless of the number of set or reps. Only the TEW single number is used to determine average monthly intensity. Even when a lesser weight is used as part of the programming, such as doing 90k x 5 x 1 and then 100k x 5 x 1, the 100k is the only value that will be considered as the TEW for that workout.

The following spreadsheet shows how the TEWs can be entered and averaged at the end of each month. The main purpose of keeping average monthly intensity is to give the lifter some idea of what their actual capacity is with respect to those averages. 80% is a good starting point, but it might need to be increased a bit or decreased a bit depending on how the lifter responds to those averages.

Date	Snatch	C&J	Back Sq	Front Sq	Sn Pull	Clean Pull
Week 1						
Mon	70%	70%	100% of C&J			
Tue	75%	70%				100% of C&J
Wed	70%	80%		90% of C&J		
Thur	80%	70%			100% of Sn	
Sat	75%	90%	120% of C&J			
Week 2						
Mon	80%	75%				95% of C&J
Tue	65%	80%		105% of C&J		
Wed	75%	75%			105% of Sn	
Thur	70%	75%	120% of C&J			
Sat	85%	70%				110% of C&J
Week 3						
Mon	80%	75%		90% of C&J		
Tue	75%	80%			100% of Sn	

Date	Snatch	C&J	Back Sq	Front Sq	Sn Pull	Clean Pull
Wed	80%	75%	100% of C&J			
Thur	80%	85%				100% of C&J
Sat	75%	90%		100% of C&J		
Week 4						
Mon	70%	80%			105% of Sn	
Tue	75%	70%	110% of C&J			
Wed	70%	80%				110% of C&J
Thur	80%	75%		95% of C&J	102.5 % of Sn	
Sat	90%	80%				
Month Ave.	76%	77.25%	110% of C&J	96% of C&J	105% of Sn	103% of C&J

Since the average monthly intensities are lower than 80% this particular month would have been a lighter month, probably after a meet or several months before a major competition. These percentages could gradually increase up to a monthly average of 80% over those several months before the peaking phase begins.

The coach or lifter can program the training and then calculate the monthly average, or weekly average from that program to make sure those average monthly percentages of the top end weights do not get out of line and stay within the 80% range.

The volume needs to be somewhat consistent so there is no substantial increase in volume due to a decrease in intensity. The lower intense workouts are primarily for the lifter to work on speed, precision and recovery, and with too much volume that can interfere in that process, thereby making the more intense workouts less effective.

There are other subsets to the top end weights that need to be included in the spreadsheet besides just the percentages or weights;

1) The overall time in motion of the snatch and clean from the platform to standing up with the weight.
2) The time in motion of when standing up out of the squat.
3) Pulls to full extension.
4) Equivalent time of the squats in 1 second and .67 seconds.

Example: A lifter does 100k snatch and 130k clean & jerk and the overall time in motion is 2.3 for the snatch and 2.4 seconds for the clean. It can be noted in the following way;

Date	Snatch	C&J	
Day 1	100k x1 (2.3)	130k x 1 (2.4)	

These times in each lift can be averaged out over the month to make sure they don't drift to far over 2.5 seconds. It is important for these times in motion to be as consistent as possible regardless of the weight. At lesser weights these times should be even faster and as each incremental increase is executed the times should gradually get slower up to the top end weight.

Example: A lifter has a PR clean of 150k and a time in motion of 2.4 seconds as a personal best. During a workout he is only able to clean & jerk 130k in 2.6 seconds. Moving slower than 2.4 seconds with less than PR should alert the lifter that he has some fatigue in the legs or back and should accommodate for that in the next workout.

Overall times can be used to evaluate the lifters ability to perform in subsequent workouts and adjustments to the top end weights can be made to accommodate the lifter, and help keep the lifter from overtraining or overreaching.

The times in the squats can be noted in the following way;

Date	Snatch	C&J	Back Squat	Equiv. in 1 sec.	Equiv. in .67
Day 1	100k x 1 (2.3)	130k x 1 (2.4)	130k x 5 x 2 @ .8	175k	142k

The above .8 seconds for the 5 sets of 2 singles is an average time in motion, but the lifter should attempt to do each rep in each set at the same .8 seconds. The equivalent of 1 second squat would be 175k and the equivalent of .67 squat from parallel would be 142k, and those equivalents can be noted on the spreadsheet in the following way.

As can be seen there is a lot more information needed about each lift other than simply the amount, reps and sets. The equivalent times also should be averaged out over the month to make sure the lifter is not overreaching. If the average equivalent times are close to 100% of the lifters equivalent time PR then the squats need to be reduced in subsequent workouts so those averages are closer to 80% average of that equivalent time PR.

Example: The same above lifter has a back squat limitation of 150k x 125% = 187.5k. This means each and every squat he performs up to 187.5k is executed in 1 second or faster. Even though these squats are 1 second they can still cause the lifter to become over trained if the monthly average is not 80% of that 187.5k = 150k for an average equivalent of 1 second.

Note: Since the times are 1 second or less, the physical recovery from overreaching is considerably less than the time it takes to recover from doing slow grinding squats on a regular basis. It might only take one or two squat workouts of approximately 50% of the lifters 1RM back squat in 1 second to physically recover. In the above case that would be 187.5k x 50% = 94k.

The pulls can be noted on the spreadsheet in the following way;

Date	Snatch	Snatch Pull	C&J	Clean Pull
Day 2	90k x 5 x 1 (2.2)	120k x 1 (.67)	120k x 3 x 2 (2.3)	140k x 4 x 2 (.63)

I am showing both snatch and clean pulls in the above example, but this might not always be the case. There are no meaningful equivalents for the pulls, as far as I have been able to determine. The times should be noted so the lifter will always be aware of their pulling velocity and that it should be the same for the competition lifts and the pulls regardless of the weight on the bar. The minute they feel they are moving slower than the .67 seconds they should halt any further increases in weight.

Since the squats and pulls are assistance lifts, it is important to realize that it's more beneficial that the snatch and clean & jerk be progressed or pushed more than the squats and pulls. This is not to say those squats and pulls should not progress, but should only be used to progress the snatch and clean & jerk. Exactly why these times in motion and equivalent times are so important for the lifter to know and understand. Assistance lifts mean that they assist the velocity of the competition lifts and they are not there to assist the squats and pulls as if they were another event.

While time in motion takes more mental concentration and precision to perform over slow grinding actions, they are less stressful on the adrenaline, muscular and neurological system, especially over the long term. Reaction times and accelerated velocities are of prime importance in nearly all sports. Moving slow in training (not during warmup periods) I believe is an irrational concept, i.e., any type of pauses during what normally would be a full movement, which includes the squats and pulls.

Section 17: The Peaking Phase

The difference between the training phase and peaking phase can be somewhat vague in the sport of weightlifting. In track and field, peaking is taken to mean being in the best shape in the most important meet of the year, whether in High School State Meets, Collegiate Nationals or World and Olympic Championships. Team sports don't contain the concept of peaking, but instead, getting into shape to begin the season forms that basic concept for team sports.

Most weightlifters come out of both team sports and individual sports where those concepts of peaking are different from sport to sport. I would consider peaking for a weightlifting meet to be much like that in track and field, where the lifter tries to peak for the most important competition they can qualify for, or in a meet where they want to achieve a qualifying total. For most lifters there is only one major championship a year where they want to do their best lifting, i.e., their State Meet, American Open or Senior Nationals. If these are the meets the lifter qualifies for then these are the meets the lifter should peak for.

Normally the lifter does not feel as much desperation or anxiety for an upcoming meet that is not a major championship. The lifter can train through local meets and not enter into a full peaking phase, but simply train down a few workouts before the meet. Expectations should be held to what the lifter has snatched or clean & jerked in the training phase. As the major meet looms closer during the training phase, the lifter might start to become anxious about their ability to perform. This is where some lifters start to push the competition lifts to maximum efforts and even to failure, as well as the squats, thinking they can gain an edge by doing so. Their performance, however, will depend more on the consistency of the weight handled, the consistency of the velocity and the precision of the lifting, with respect to the primary lifts executed during the training process for the meet.

Peaking Phase: Average Monthly Intensities

The following schedule is similar to the previous training phase schedule, except there are more lifts that exceed 90%, even though the average intensity level is still maintained at 80%. The snatch and clean & jerk should be alternating intensity levels instead of doing both lifts at the same level of intensity on the same day. This done primarily to keep from overtraining or allowing too much fatigue to set in for subsequent workouts. The squats and pulls are excluded from this schedule.

Date	Snatch	Clean & Jerk
1st Week		
Mon	80%	70%
Tue	75%	80%
Wed	85%	80%
Thurs	80%	75%
Sat	95%	80%
2nd Week		
Mon	70%	85%

Date	Snatch	Clean & Jerk
Tue	75%	75%
Wed	80%	85%
Thurs	75%	80%
Sat	80%	95%
3rd Week		
Mon	80%	70%
Tue	75%	85%
Wed	85%	80%
Thurs	80%	75%
Sat	100%	80%
4th Week		
Mon	70%	85%
Tue	80%	80%
Wed	80%	85%
Thurs	75%	75%
Sat	75%	100%
Monthly Ave.	79.75%	81%

In the above hypothetical peaking phase schedule the average monthly intensity was kept at 80%, in order to allow for the higher intensity levels on Saturday (meet day normally) for the snatch or clean & jerk, but not both. Again the average monthly intensity levels for the top end weights should be greater for the clean & jerk, and the snatch should be the same as the clean & jerk but never greater, at least over a one month cycle.

The pulls should never exceed 100% of snatch or clean & jerk during the peaking phase so each and every pull will be executed at the right velocity to full extension. A reduction in volume is also recommended.

The squats will stay the same as they were during the training phase. There can be some slight increase in intensity, but only if those squats are achieved within the particular time in motion allowed.

Reps would be reflected in the percentages, i.e., 70% to 75% might reflect triples or doubles, 75% to 80% might reflect doubles and anything over 80% would reflect singles, although this would be left up to the judgement of the lifter or their coach.

If the lifter is unable to lift 95% to 100% on any particular Saturday, then the following week should be somewhat less intense in order for the lifter to recover to where they can lift 95% or more, without missing, and with some precision and particular times in motion, i.e., 2.5 seconds overall time in motion for the snatch and clean. It will not do the lifter much good if they have to grind out of their snatch or clean during the peaking phase, and especially if they miss those lifts the first attempt and then make them on the second or third attempt.

When alternating the snatch and clean & jerk from week to week, the peaking phase might need to last two months to give the lifter time to get in enough near maximum lifts with precision and speed, to hone in those lifts at the precise level they need them to be in order to compete at their best.

Average levels of intensity can be different for lifters depending on their level of proficiency. A professional lifter could easily handle average monthly intensities of 85%, and possibly more, but a beginner would be foolish to attempt anything more than 80% and in some cases 75%. Non professional lifters should stay around 80% for both the training and peaking phase.

During the training phase the 80% average monthly intensity will be composed of high end weights between 75% and 85% for the majority of the time and during the shorter peaking phase the high end weights will be between 65% and 95%. The greater difference in percentages allows for those 95% lifts during the peaking phase, yet still hold the monthly level of intensity to 80%. The 80% forms the basis for consistency in the overall intensity and helps keep the lifter from overtraining as long as the volume is held to those levels which also keep the lifter from overtraining.

Section 18: Miscellaneous Topics

Manipulating Intensities in the Primary Lifts

There are four general classifications of resistance;

1) Recovery - from the empty bar up to 69% of PR
2) Training - from 70% to 85% of PR
3) Peaking - from 86% to 100%

The level of resistance in the recovery category is reserved for pre-warmup weights, recovery sessions, active rest sessions and pre-training or conditioning phases. The training category of resistance are weights used during the training phase where the lifter is preparing for the peaking phase and the competition.

During the training phase the intensity can be manipulated between 75% and 85% depending on the session and what the lifter wants to accomplish. When doing doubles the intensity might need to be reduced to less than 85%, the same for doing cleans + 1 + 1 or clean + 2 jerks, etc.

If doubles or triples are being scheduled then in order for the 85% to be maintained the sets of reps should always be less than 85%. In order to snatch in doubles or triples the intensity has to be commensurate with the precision and time in motion requirements of each rep in every set up to the top end weight. The same for the clean + 2 jerks as well as the back squat. The lifter must know they can achieve those lifts and if there is any doubt they should reduce the intensity so those requirements can be met.

The snatch and clean & jerk needs to be limited by precision and the 2.5 second time in motion, and the 80% monthly limitation, in order for the squats and pulls to remain energetic, and for the snatch and clean & jerk to stay honed in so the lifter can peak properly for meets.

Any additional volume of snatches and clean & jerks requires the intensity to be reduced commensurate with the precision and velocity that needs to be achieved. The clean pull is less restricted by the .67 time than the 1 second time for the squats, but for the majority of training and during the peaking phase, the pulls should be executed at .67 second time in motion regardless of the amount of weight the lifter is able to handle.

Example: If a lifter can snatch 150k and the time in motion from the platform to full extension is .67 seconds, but all he can snatch pull in .67 seconds is 140k, then 140k should be the limitation and he should attempt to do less weight faster until the 150k snatch pull can be achieved in .67 seconds.

Pre packaged programs are not practical or workable over long periods of time, such as a month or more. Only a lifter or coach can know how much volume and what intensity levels should be achieved in any particular session. The order of the lifts should be non-negotiable with the snatch and clean & jerk coming before the squats or pulls for the vast majority of training and with few exceptions. The squats can come first in a morning session where less intensity is being planned for the snatch and clean & jerk. The regular training sessions should always place the squats after the snatch and/or clean & jerk. Doing squats first during a regular session where the snatch and clean &

jerk are being executed at 85% or more should be avoided. The normal thought process is that by squatting first the snatch will be disadvantaged due to some fatigue, however, it is more important to execute the snatch with speed and precision, and this is hard to do from a point of fatigue. The main point would be that no one ever does squats as a warmup during a weightlifting meet.

The only purpose of the squats and pulls is to assist the lifter with the 1st pull and recovery and for the jerk drive, as well as additional stability when receiving the weight. The squats and pulls are not simply for setting PRs for the sake of PRs by engaging in some sort of squat or pull routine or strength cycle. The squats and pulls need to follow the incremental increases from the clean & jerk so those incremental increases establish a link between the comp lifts and the squats and pulls. If these lifts are not linked together the correlation between lift to squat can become increasingly meaningless or at least difficult to determine.

Occasional variations to the order of lifts is fine as long as it is occasional and does not become over extended, such as doing the squats first for several weeks. There should be plenty of variations between the primary lifts themselves to continue to keep the order of lifts as a constant. Another reason for this is so it becomes easier to tell how gains were made and so adjustments to the volume and intensity can be achieved as needed. If training becomes too varied it can be very difficult to know how or why progress was made or not made.

Philosophical Concept of Precision and Velocity

The fast twitch muscle fiber's cell growth (hypertrophy) should be increased through specific velocities (times in motion). Moving at specific velocities increases the fast twitch cell growth and moving slower increases the slow twitch cell growth. If the slow twitch fibers are increased more than the fast twitch, then that can be a nullification in the fast twitch fibers ability to move quicker. Generally I like to believe it more important to move faster regardless of which fibers are being increased. The biomechanics of motion and the physics are the same, but instead of talking about how the different muscles behave it might be better to understand the physics of how those muscles need to behave.

Being precise in each and every lift cannot come at the expense of moving slower or more cautious in an attempt to be precise. At each and every incremental increase both precision and velocity must be maximized. Specifically, any attempt over 50% must be maximized at 100% effort. It is far better to miss lifts due to moving too fast than too slow. A technical error is not as costly as an error in velocity, as far as training is concerned. Precision and moving at specific velocities should not be thought of as separate elements, but ingrained as a whole. Technique, precision and specific velocities should also be ingrained as a whole. Even if technique is perfect, but the time in motion is slower than 2.5 seconds, then the lift should not be considered a perfectly executed lift. The lifter's proficiency, and their ability to generate specific velocities needs to be linked together for the lifter to continue to progress at a consistent level and that progress not become slowed or halted.

If the overall time in motion of the clean is trained at slower than 2.5 second velocities, the progress of the lifter is also slowed, until the lifter is unable to make any more progress at all. This would be in cases where the clean is achieved in 3 seconds or slower at the top end weights. Some slight improvement in performance can be achieved between 2.5 seconds and 3 seconds, but progress will still be slower than if all those cleans were achieved in 2.5 seconds or faster. The slower the overall times in motion are then the slower the progress will be.

Slower overall times in motion in the clean & jerk are caused by slower times in the squats and pulls. The squats and pulls are linked to the snatch and clean & jerk and are not separate elements. How the squats and pulls are executed will be reflected back to the snatch and clean & jerk, primarily in the 1st pull and recovery and the dip and drive of the jerk.

The amount of weight on the bar in the squats and pulls is irrelevant if the squats and pulls are executed at slower times than those needed to keep the bidirectional velocities in the snatch and clean & jerk in agreement. It is not possible to just try and move fast, the actual times in motion of the top end weights must be measured during each training session or filmed and then measured after each session.

It could be a monumental waste of time to go into the gym and train using slower times in motion. The volume has to become greater and the time spent training has to become longer to make up for the slower velocities. As long as the lifter can move at the optimum times in motion with precision, then training can last as long as those times and precision are maintained. If training continues on past the point where the times in motion and precision begin to degrade, and the longer this goes on, the quicker the lifter will reach stagnation or become overtrained.

A lifter cannot train long hours and multiple sessions, yet move at slower times in motion, and expect the same results as maintaining faster overall times in motion regardless of the volume, frequency or length of training.

There is nothing in the long list of common sense understandings that would suggest that moving slower has any validity in athletics in any phase of training for any reason whatsoever.

Each individual lifter should be patently aware of the velocities and times in motion needed for each lift. And those times must be ingrained so the lifter will know when they have reached their peak performance in training when going up incrementally to their top end weights. Times in motion cannot have a large statistical deviation, but need to be within a relatively small range of acceptable parameters.

A lifter who can clean & jerk 150k in training on a consistent basis, but the overall time in motion is 3 seconds instead of 2.5 seconds, needs to make a decision to keep training at the same velocity or reduce the weight so the times in motion are 2.5 seconds, and not increase the weight until they can do more at the same 2.5 seconds overall time. Obviously a similar decision has to be made with respect to the squats and pulls in order for those times to be in agreement with the 2.5 second time, because the squats and pulls are inescapably linked to the snatch and clean & jerk and are *not* auxiliary exercises or separate events.

The technique, velocity and precision of the squats and pulls must be held to the exact same standards as those squats and pulls contained in the snatch and clean & jerk. The same logical conclusion should be arrived at, with respect to technique in the snatch or clean & jerk, as arrived at with respect to the squats and pulls. Lifters should not talk about how fast a lifter can move in the snatch or clean & jerk and yet not talk about how fast they move in the squats and pulls. It's always, and incorrectly reasoned, about numbers in the squats and pulls and about velocity or speed or quickness in the snatch and clean & jerk. This separation of reasoning between numbers and velocity is illogical. If all that mattered was how much a lifter could squat or pull (dead lift) then why train the competition lifts at all, why not just train the squat and dead lift as in powerlifting and only do the snatch and clean & jerk in the meets. This would never work, nor would only doing the snatch and clean & jerk and not doing squats or pulls, because the primary lifts are inseparably linked to one another and need to be trained similarly and as one unit in order to progress all the primary lifts together toward full potential.

Section 19: Conclusion

All athletes are conditioned to train their skills using quick reaction times, which can be related to specific times in motion. No athlete, especially in individual sports, can train by moving slower than what is ultimately required of them to progress their performance. It is very difficult to train the muscular system to move slow and then call on it to increase the accelerated velocity. It is much easier and more efficient to train the muscular system to move as fast as possible and then slow down just enough to control those changes in acceleration during the transitional phases.

Do weightlifters have to be strong? I suppose, but the word strength has to be quantified as to it's meaning before any assumption or conclusion can be drawn for the usage of the word "strength". Strength is the ability of an object or person to withstand forces placed on that object or person. Overcoming and producing force requires that object or person to be in motion and the faster the change in acceleration then more force can be overcome and produced, therefore, moving slower produces less force. The same logic must be applied to moving slower in the squats and pulls, which would also produce less force. The challenge for the weightlifter is keeping the accelerated velocities (time in motion) in those squats and pulls at the right velocity (t) which will benefit the bidirectional motions of the snatch and clean & jerk. As long as gains in the squats and pulls contains those same velocities needed in the bidirectional motions of the snatch and clean & jerk, then that would be considered being stronger. Lifting to absolute failure on a consistent basis, in the primary lifts, does not produce a stronger lifter, but a slower lifter and one that is more susceptible to becoming erratic and less efficient.

How much weight a lifter should handle in training the competition lifts is tied to specific times in motion, and not just to the amount of weight that can be moved without regard to those specific times. I believe that 85% of PR is that limit where precision and optimum times in motion are best achieved during training phases. The squats and pulls are no different in this regard, and should be trained using limitations of 125% for the back squat and 110% for the front squat and thereby keeping the velocity levels at 1 second or faster. Moving more weight slower does nothing but overload the muscular system and work the slow twitch to the point of decreasing the lifter's ability to move at the optimum times in motion during the changes in direction.

The top lifters in the world do not move faster because they can squat and pull more weight slower. The same accelerated velocities used in the snatch and clean & jerk are used in the squats and pulls. There is some leeway as regards to how fast the squats and pulls should be executed. On occasion, times of 1.1 to 1.5 seconds in the squats might be acceptable, but only on rare occasions when it can't be helped, but not for the vast majority of training. The main point is to not allow the weight to decelerate during the recovery of the squat or clean and during the pulls, and especially the jerk drive. The 1 second recovery time eliminates any deceleration, which cannot be said conclusively for slower than 1 second times.

It might seem like increasing the performance of the squats and pulls cannot be achieved by moving at 1 second all the time, but it only seems that way. The reality is that any lift can be progressed from any point of origin. Using absolute strength methods, where the velocity is not regarded, is a faster way to increase performance, but it's also a faster way to reach stagnation. Heavier and slower squats and pulls supersedes the bidirectional motions ability to use those type of squats and pulls, because the velocities don't match up, and the 1st pull and recovery become slower, which causes the overall time in motion of the snatch and clean to become slower.

Only from video can actual determinations be made, when times are not noticeably slower, as to whether the lifter decelerated during the recovery or during the 1st pull, however, it can be readily seen if the lifter is dragging the weight off the platform in the 1st pull, and the recovery is a grinding effort. The lifter at this point will find it more difficult to increase their performance and normally blame it on not being able to squat more weight. The real problem is not squatting more weight slower, but squatting the right amount of weight faster or in 1 second. It actually does not matter what the relationship is between the squats and clean & jerk as long as the squats are trained at 1 second in the recovery. The correct correlation to the clean & jerk will seek the right ratio over time. This being far better than trying to increase the squats or pulls using slow grinding motions and using powerlifting type squat routines.

The proof is in the pudding, so to speak, and following is a list of some top lifters and their times in motion in the clean during competition.

Hossein Rezazadeh (105k+) of Iran 263.5k, 2004 Olympics
Platform to knees .30 seconds
Front Squat Recovery .77 seconds
Overall Time in motion 2.13 seconds

Dmitry Klokov (105k) of Russia 232k, 2011 World Championships
Platform to knees .33 seconds
Front Squat Recovery .90 seconds
Overall Time in motion 2.1 seconds

Khadzhimurat Akkaev (105k) of Russia, 232k, 2011 World Championships
Platform to knees .30 seconds
Front Squat Recovery 1 second
Overall Time in motion 2.3 seconds

Ilya Ilyin (94k) of Kazakhstan, 233k, 2012 Olympics
Platform to knees .30 seconds
Front Squat Recovery 1 second
Overall Time in motion 2.3 seconds

Lu Xiaojun (77k) of China, 204k, 2013 World Championships
Platform to knees .30 seconds
Front Squat Recovery .80 seconds
Overall Time in motion 2.1 seconds

Apti Aukhadov (85k) of Russia, 215k, 2013 Europeans
Platform to knees .33 seconds
Front Squat Recovery .80 seconds
Overall Time in motion 2.1 seconds

Pyrros Dimas (90k) of Greece, 211k, 1995 World Championships
Platform to knees .30 seconds
Front Squat Recovery .80 seconds
Overall Time in motion 2 seconds

This list could be almost endless as regards to the top lifters, past or present. Also their back and front squats were measured at 1 to 1.3 seconds in the recovery. They rarely if ever attempt maximum efforts at slow grinding times of motion. In fact, if you ask most top lifters how much they can squat, they will reply they don't know, because they never tried a maximal squat. Outside the classification of top level the overall times in motion tend to drop off gradually, but most of the lifters in the A session of the World Championships are around 2.5 seconds or faster. There is a drop off in time gradually on average as the proficiency of the lifter drops off.

The faster overall times in motion are a result of receiving the clean at parallel, and the snatch in the full squat position, which cuts down the time in motion considerably over receiving the weight and riding it down, even a small amount riding the weight down can add up to .5 seconds to the overall time. It is undetermined what part the stature of the lifter played in the overall times. What cannot be disputed is the faster overall times set the lifter up for an easier jerk attempt, as less energy is expended during the clean. It also conserves energy to use a timed rebound in the snatch as well as the clean.

The amount of weight is relative to all lifters, beginner or elite levels. A world record or 100k PR clean & jerk is the same and should generally take the same amount of time to execute. Any discrepancy with slower times would mean the lifter is not training the squats and pulls correctly or with enough velocity or they are not receiving the bar at the lowest possible trajectory point and/or other technical deviations.

I have tried to develop a general methodology for how training should be conducted in the sport of weightlifting in order to achieve full potential. While some programs offer a different course of action, that course must still be based on the primary lifts first and foremost, otherwise the lifter is simply engaging in an exercise regime, which happens to include the snatch and clean & jerk. Developing a particular physique or trying to become fit should be well outside the scope of what training for weightlifting is all about.

How long or hard a lifter trains has no meaning if that training is not carried out correctly. At which point, training 6 days a week twice a day will only get the lifter in shape to train that amount of time, but might not do anything to progress them to full potential. Doing mainly jerks out of the rack and just cleans will not get the lifter into shape, only the clean & jerk can do that. Doing complex combinations will only get the lifter into shape for doing complex combinations. Doing overhead squats will only get the lifter in shape for overhead squats. Doing squat routines will only get the lifter in shape for those squat routines.

Trying to vary the workouts through inclusions of certain auxiliary exercises can be antagonistic to the overall development of the lifter, when those auxiliary exercises are pushed to the same levels of intensity as the primary lifts. The concept of developing the core of the athlete through specialized auxiliary exercises has little or no bearing on increasing performance. The core must be developed through the primary lifts and primarily through those primary lifts. Variations to training should go through the primary lifts, by manipulating the volume, intensity, frequency (rest or recovery periods) and using those variations which can be achieved when lifting off the platform, such as not moving the feet, changing the grip and/or receiving the weight at different heights.

Lifting off boxes and from the hang in order to save the legs is preposterous. The 1st pull is the most important phase of the lift and needs to be executed as much as possible during training and lifting off boxes and from the hang should never be executed in leu of the full movement or in excess of those full movements.

The squats and pulls are not strength lifts per se, at least in the common vernacular of what the word strength means to most lifters. The squats and pulls are a continuation of the incremental increases of the clean & jerk including those same specific velocities as the snatch and clean & jerk. The squats and pulls have to be linked to the competition lifts and should not be trained as separate lifts. To view the squats and pulls as separate lifts will do little more than cause those lifts to become another event or be trained too often and with too much intensity with respect to the competition lifts. Proportionality between all the primary lifts has to be maintained through precision and specific times in motion in order to continue to increase performance.

If squatting and pulling more weight slower is considered being strong, then the lifter is becoming a powerlifter who knows how to snatch and clean & jerk. Their primary emphasis is switched from the snatch and clean & jerk to the squats and dead lifts and over time both the lifts and power lifts will become mediocre as a whole.

The powerlifting approach will not develop full potential, it's impossible. Full potential can only be achieved by adhering to specific times in motion and becoming very precise in the technical aspects of all the primary lifts. In other words, the weightlifter must train like athletes in other individual sports, such as track & field, swimming, etc., and not like powerlifters, bodybuilders, strongmen or exercise buffs. The desire and determination to overcome the pain threshold can only be triggered through the specific events of the weightlifter, and nothing else can or will progress the lifter to full potential.

As a lifter weaves their way through the different levels of performance from beginner to elite lifter, and for some, master lifter, the times in motion of all the primary lifts must stay consistent and not overly vary. The top end weights must also be consistent in weight, and achieved with precision. There is no other way a weightlifter can progress to their full potential. All the growling, loud music, motivational blather, bar slamming and PR chasing has no effect on making gains over long periods of time, because the lifter will eventually burn out well before full potential is reached. Athletes should stay calm and collected during training and even between sessions.

Athletics requires a special kind of discipline, and behavior. To reach full potential the lifter must be able to internalize their struggle. They must visualize their potential and strive to find ways to reach that potential. This internalized struggle is never finished, until the athlete has given all they have, and at the end of their career they know deep down they achieved all they could have achieved with all the knowledge and experience both athlete and coach possesed.

Made in the USA
San Bernardino, CA
15 May 2017